BOOST
YOUR
CAREER

BOOST YOUR CAREER

HOW TO MAKE AN IMPACT, GET RECOGNIZED, AND BUILD THE CAREER YOU WANT

SANDER AND MECHELE FLAUM

ALLWORTH PRESS

Allworth Press books may be purchased in bulk at special discounts for sales promotion, corporate gifts, fund-raising, or educational purposes. Special editions can also be created to specifications. For details, contact the Special Sales Department, Allworth Press, 307 West 36th Street, 11th Floor, New York, NY 10018 or info@skyhorsepublishing.com.

20 19 18 17   5 4 3 2 1

Published by Allworth Press, an imprint of Skyhorse Publishing, Inc.
307 West 36th Street, 11th Floor, New York, NY 10018.

Allworth Press® is a registered trademark of Skyhorse Publishing, Inc.®, a Delaware corporation.

www.allworth.com

Cover design by Mary Ann Smith

Library of Congress Cataloging-in-Publication Data is available on file.

Print ISBN: 978-1-62153-569-0
Ebook ISBN: 978-1-62153-572-0

Printed in the United States of America

"Unless you try to do something beyond what you have already mastered, you will never grow."

—Ralph Waldo Emerson

This book is dedicated to dear friends and true leaders,
the late Senator John Glenn, and Annie Glenn,
his wonderful wife of seventy-three years.

Contents

Foreword

ONE OF THE MOST VALUABLE PIECES OF career advice I have ever received came from John H. Johnson, an African American businessman in Chicago. You may know him for memorably launching his empire—which included *Ebony* and *Jet* magazines—in his youth in the 1940s with a $500 loan secured by his mother's furniture. He became the first African American to make *Forbes* magazine's list of the four hundred wealthiest Americans. I wanted to meet this guy.

I wanted to hear what advice he would offer to a young person who was starting out—as I was—and trying to make it in the career world. His advice was well crafted and succinct.

Just three words: "Make yourself indispensable," he said.

Make yourself the first person who comes to your boss's mind when a tough job has to be done. If the structure is not there to fill the need, create it yourself. Detect a need and do your best to fill it, not just well but *irreplaceably*. Even in hard times, make yourself the last person that your employers would even think about letting go. Johnson did that. He saw a national market of literate and employed African Americans who were not being serviced by the highly segregated media of those times—and he serviced that demand.

The world and its media have changed tremendously since those days. Yet the value of Johnson's advice—"Make yourself indispensable"—to new generations in rapidly changing times is as relevant as ever.

Johnson's advice came back to mind as I was reading this book by Sander Flaum and Mechele Flaum. *Boost Your Career* aims to help you—and me—to make ourselves indispensable. It expands and updates the spirit of Johnson's advice in many ways, with pointed advice for those who are wondering where to go from here with their careers—and how to get there.

Many people spend years working long hours yet find themselves spinning their wheels—passed over for promotions, recognition, and pay raises—and clueless to the hidden rules that, despite their usefulness, almost never get taught in classrooms.

One of the most important of these ingredients for success is what Sander and Mechele Flaum call "meaningful impact" projects; these impact projects make a striking difference in an organization in ways that make an employee stand out in the eyes of key stakeholders and fellow employees. Drawing on their many years in business in a variety of high-level roles—plus interviews with dozens of other successful executives—the Flaums show the best ways to identify opportunities, set goals, and take leadership in projects that will help employees and their organizations achieve those goals.

"Impact work," as the Flaum's call work that aims to impress those individuals who can help your advancement, has four crucial "pillars" that the Flaums describe in chapter 1:

One, determine who your real boss—or bosses—happen to be. In most organizations, the lines of real day-to-day influence are not always spelled out on the organizational chart. Closer examination reveals other individuals who may be at your same organizational level or even in another department, yet they exert enough influence that their support is worth pursuing. This chapter tells why.

Two, keep it simple. The simplest changes and innovations often work best. Following this advice will save you from the heartache of exhaustive efforts that bring disappointingly little, if any, reward. This chapter shows how to "play to your strengths," avoid wasting time, and work more efficiently.

Three, don't be afraid to change. It's "your friend," say the Flaums. That's easier advice for many of us to believe than to follow. We often don't realize how comfortable our comfort zones have become until change forces us out of them. Get over the shock of change and try to get in front of it—so you can take the best advantage of it.

Four, when all those pillars are built—then you can innovate.

The book takes a deep dive into those four pillars of success and isolates other important commandments for the savvy employee to which we too often pay too little attention, such as:

- Leverage your passions.
- Set clear expectations.
- Consider a timeline to be a promise.
- Preserve team synergy.

And there's the always tricky but critical commandment that reminds me of a Kenny Rogers song: "Know when to fold."

There are two kinds of people in this world, my father advised. There are the "movers and shakers," and there are those who "get moved and shaken." The difference between those two classes in today's world is a proper education. This book aims to help you to be a mover and shaker, no matter how much you may have been moved and shaken.

—Clarence Page
March 2017

INTRODUCTION
Get the Boost You Need

HAVE YOU BEEN WORKING YOUR BUTT OFF, yet you never receive that promotion, recognition, or pay raise you crave? Maybe you go in early, stay late, and have dedicated years to doing your best. Perhaps you're just starting out in a new position and want to seize every chance to succeed. If you want to launch into the next level of your career, this book is for you.

Don't be the person who works hard but isn't considered leader material. Don't let the corporate culture stand in your way. Don't give in to departmental angst or watch your coworkers "magically" become the go-to gal or guy instead of you. Yes, skilled people get overlooked in the workplace. Talented people get ignored. Heck, even ambitious people stagnate. If you want to be the one they send in to throw the Hail Mary pass, even the one to call the play, you need to demonstrate that you can do it. You do that by focusing on the right things.

I guarantee you, there are untapped opportunities in your company. Being able to identify those opportunities is what makes all the difference. This isn't just about working harder—it's about working smarter. To make a resounding impact in an organization, you need to immediately elevate executives' perceptions of you and you need to know what type of work gets noticed.

During the past fifty years, I've worked as a corporate marketing head, advertising agency CEO, and C-suite consultant. I founded and grew a successful marketing and sales business that advises executives in a variety of capacities. My coauthor and wife, Mechele Flaum, has worked in marketing for almost forty years consulting with leading organizations in a variety of industries. She founded and manages her own firm that advises clients on marketing strategy and consumer trends.

Through working with many hundreds of people in Fortune 500, established, and entrepreneurial organizations, we've seen many careers soar while others fizzle out. What most often separates these people isn't intelligence or drive—it is the ability to successfully navigate workplace culture, build the right relationships, and get noticed for doing things that matter to stakeholders.

Time and time again, we've seen this hold true. It became clear to us that there was a need to state the modern-day, unwritten rules for getting ahead. Impressing the right people and getting noticed are essential in today's workplace, where employees are judged in real time. This book will help you transform *how* you work, while changing key players' perceptions of your capabilities.

Set Your Destination

You may have picked up this book knowing specifically what you want to achieve. You may have your future title, responsibilities, or salary number in mind. Or you may vaguely know you want something different, better, more respected, more valued in your organization. It's essential to enter the journey that this book will take you on by clarifying your personal and professional goals. So take the time now to write them down somewhere.

After writing down the more surface aspect, like a raise or promotion, drill deep. We want to challenge you to think about *why* you want these things. What is your emotional investment in achieving this? What satisfaction will it give you on a deep, inner level? For example, you may ultimately want a promotion to team lead. On an inner level, you want to earn this through your exemplary performance. If so, your goals need to include demonstrating your passion for the company's mission, exhibiting your specialized skills, and doing so in a way that inspires others.

Clarifying your desired outcomes in this way, from the get-go, will make it much easier to understand the types of relationships and projects that will help you reach your goals. You can refer to these goals as you absorb the advice in this book and apply it directly to achieving them. Later in your journey, you'll also be better able to measure your accomplishments and impact.

NEW RULES FOR A NEW WORKPLACE

If you're like many people today, you feel confused about how to boost your career because the status quo has changed. The working world is in constant flux. Rules from forty, twenty, and even ten years ago don't apply today. So your father's advice won't translate. Even the things that worked for your big sister may not be relevant any more. And if you're trying to apply the same strategy that you got you where you are today, you're not likely to reach the next rung. The world changes in a blink, and how we work also changes. That's why we need to stay dynamic.

It's hard to see things evolve in real time, but with an opportunity to step back and compare, the differences are vast. Mechele saves good business articles, and she has an impressive collection that goes back many years. Flipping through those pieces is like opening a time capsule, and it gives us the chance to see business dynamism at play. One twenty-year-old article about how young people don't prepare properly for job interviews featured the story of a recent college grad who applied for an entry-level job at a national cookie company. The hopeful hire came up with a new concept for a cookie, baked some at home, and brought them to the interview. The managers who interviewed her were appalled. Without permission or knowing the machinery, process, or legal issues about product liability, she had the audacity to bring a home-baked, "improved" version of their product to an interview. This was an example of what not to do.

That was twenty years ago. If she had brought that plateful of cookies to an interview today, she'd have the job. Hiring managers would commend her creativity, problem-solving, proactive approach, appetite for taking smart risks, and knowledge of what it takes to bake. She would stand memorably apart from cookieless contenders. This shows how the value for entrepreneurial drive and ingenuity has shifted in a notable way, and how employees are judged differently today than they were in the past. With new technology and new generations in the workplace, getting ahead requires an ever-fresh state of mind. This book will show you how to stay alert for opportunities, no matter what the future holds.

YOU'RE THE BEST ADVANTAGE YOU HAVE

It's up to you to take the reins to getting ahead. And it requires urgency. Because if you're not busy building the career you crave, you've probably settled into a ditch where promotion is unlikely. If you're stagnant, plodding along in the same role you were initially hired into the company for, haven't been bumped up to higher positions, and get ignored when more responsibilities are being divvied, those are signs that you are not ready to be recognized and moved up. You have work to do, because the hard truth is that it's not up to your managers to recognize your potential—it's up to you to show them what you've got.

It's common for high-risers to shoot up fast. This may have even happened to you: you landed an entry-level position and immediately stood out as a future star. Within a year, or even more quickly, you were bumped up to the next level or received feedback that you're on the way up. This continued until, inevitably, two rising stars were competing for the same slot. Then someone got the short straw, possibly for the first time in his or her life. If this happened to you, it's a shock. And it hurts.

Both of these situations are challenging but not impossible to fix. The answer lies in you. You are the best advantage you have. It is *your* responsibility to show why you are a winner, a "must keep," even a secret weapon for your organization. You won't win points for putting in your time, doing the work that is assigned to you, and hoping someone notices. That strategy may have worked years ago, but today, that mentality makes employees average at best. It's time to think and act big! In these pages, you will find many ways to prove you belong in bigger shoes.

REAL-TIME PERFORMANCE EVALUATIONS

Being watched and measured by your company isn't creepy when you make it work for you. Organizations and managers used to give employees time to prove themselves, but you no longer have the luxury of pursuing success at a leisurely pace. Yearly performance reviews were once standard, but companies are beginning to think they are antiquated. So many things change in the course of a year, and annually conducting lengthy reviews is a burden and time suck for everyone. Organizations, in a variety of industries, are switching to biannual or quarterly reviews. Some are even doing away with formal performance reviews altogether and are instead evaluating employees on a continuous basis—in real time.

New software makes it possible for companies to monitor employees' successes through a variety of metrics. For example, Kimberly-Clark is a company known to employ lifelong workers. Now it is using a cloud-based system that gives employees personalized, data-backed goals, then tracks their progress and the amount of time it takes to meet the goal. Executives are using this as a tool for "managing out the deadwood": the employees who are not constantly showing improved metrics. This change has resulted in doubling the combined voluntary and forced turnover rate in the past ten years.[1]

This type of technology also makes it easy to draw comparisons between employees, which is creating more competitive working environments. Such systems are still in the early adoption phase, but trust me, they are on the horizon and just one aspect of the trend to ask "What have you done for me lately?" In this new normal, it's essential to not only be productive but to be productive in the ways that matter.

THE THINGS THAT MATTER TO THE PEOPLE WHO MATTER

The working world is complex—priorities vary between companies, departments, and individual managers. Employees do receive a fair amount of direction about what the large-scale priorities are. They know the company's values, its product or service, and the competitive advantage they need to uphold. Beyond that, it's up to you to decipher. Your boss wants you to deliver on what you were hired to do, but what's truly important to your boss? Does she want a collaborative, think-tank-style team? Maybe she needs efficiency and quick turnarounds. Perhaps she needs the next big idea to take upward. Or she could use some help slimming the departmental budget. That's for you to find out, and when you do, it can make all the difference.

Your boss is just one example of how navigating the work environment depends on connecting with the people who are most influential to your success and understanding what drives them. These motivational factors aren't written anywhere, so the only ways to figure them out are through talking to people, listening to what they say and applying it, or trial and error. If you're lucky, people will be candid about their personal likes and dislikes. "I'm a stickler for organization." Or a colleague might give you a helpful heads-up: "Mr. Thompson loves it when people are self-propelled executers, so be sure to put together a meeting agenda and email it to everyone two days before." This type of information is crucial for getting ahead because it shows how Mr. Thompson, a stakeholder in your career advancement, views success. You might consider yourself organized, but after learning how much he values this trait, your mission is to make those skills shine. On the flip side, you also know a quick way to irritate him—so at the very least pull together that agenda. At the most, see his preference as an opportunity to hold the most productive meeting possible and include clear-as-a-bell talking points so invitees can be even better prepared.

Little nuggets like this draw executive attention. They empower you with information that helps you adapt your work style in ways that could prove vital to your success. Before you started working with Mr. Thompson's team, maybe you didn't see the value in creating meeting agendas and sharing them in advance. Maybe you didn't even think of doing it. But now you not only know that your time is well spent because it's important to Mr. Thompson, but you also see why it's important to him. As you continue to work with him, your organizational skills can be the advantage that builds your relationship. He will trust you because you make his job easier.

Whether Mr. Thompson is your manager, client, or CEO, if he's in your corner you have a better shot at advancement. The reason? You are building an all-important emotional connection—a key factor in boosting your career. With all of this in mind, you can see how delivering the things that matter to the people who matter is essential. Throughout this book, we will offer tips for reaching out in ways that benefit everyone, especially you.

PUT RELATIONSHIPS AT THE CORE
OF YOUR EFFORTS

Faith Popcorn, an industry-leading futurist, says that the importance of cultivating professional relationships is a trend that's here to stay. When she lectured to my MBA leadership course at the Fordham Gabelli Graduate School of Business, she said, "There's a wonderful expression: *It's not what you know, it's who you know.* I want to tell you that it's so true." She told the class that while knowledge and education are definitely crucial for success, we should never downplay the power of relationships. "The likability factor is important in business. It matters how much people like you. Not because you're sucking up to them, but because you go out of your way for them and you are authentic."[2] Popcorn has again and again demonstrated her ability to predict movements in the business world, including the things that are evergreen. She also happens to be Mechele's sister.

The thing is, it's really hard to teach anyone how to build relationships and improve likability. But since you are avid about boosting your career, know this: you need to emphasize relationships and likeability as the most important work you can do—because you are almost always doing work for somebody. You need to build strong emotional connections with your coworkers, manager, executives, teams in other departments, or even a group working on the other side of the world. If other people have that connection and you don't, you will watch them fly right by you. That's why this book is packed with advice for developing positive interpersonal exchanges.

At the heart of all your efforts to boost your career is emotional intelligence, known as EQ. This is the ability to recognize your own emotions and other people's emotions—and then use that information to guide your thinking and doing. Psychologist and author Daniel Goleman developed this quotient as a skill that can be honed.

Your EQ is measured by five key competencies: self-awareness, self-regulation, social skill, empathy, and motivation. To excel in these areas is to have a high EQ, which studies have linked to a variety of career-boosting outcomes, including better relationships at work and being perceived more positively by others.[3] Fortunately, all of the EQ competencies are skills that can be developed with hard work, training, reflection, and candid feedback. By improving your EQ, you will better understand yourself and everyone around you. This empowers you to cultivate emotional connections with people much more easily—especially those who have a different work style than you, who value things you never considered, and who do things in ways that previously baffled you. Because we work so collaboratively today, developing this skillset is essential and provides the foundation for all the relationship advice in this book.

Having high EQ leads to insights like this one, which addresses how to navigate politics in a workplace where competition is unavoidable. Dr. Cameron Durrant, chairman and CEO of KaloBios, shared some great advice with me and the class on keeping the right state of mind. "Sometimes politicking happens because people think, 'Okay, the pie is only this big. More for you is less for me.' A better perspective is, 'How do we collectively bake a bigger pie, so more for me is more for you as well?'"[4]

This is the basic mindset that you need to keep in all your efforts to boost you career. You don't need to bring other people down to bring yourself up. Instead, base everything on the belief that getting ahead is about making other people look good, whether they're your clients, your boss, or your direct reports. We'll get really specific about ways to do this in chapter 2, "Fuel Up with the Support You Need." The paradox of success is that you get ahead by never making it about you—and always making it about them. Creating value for others is how you show your own value.

DRAW ON YOUR VARIETY

While working with others' benefits in mind may be a simple theory, putting it into action can be tricky. How do you identify what your colleagues and clients will find valuable? We will delve into that topic in the following chapters, but it's important to know up front that providing long-term value to a variety of people means broadening your knowledge, experience, and skillset. A recent study found that gaining experience in different business functions greatly increases the likelihood of obtaining an executive position. For example, a person who works in project management for years has a lower chance of becoming a top executive than someone who worked in project management but also spent time in another department, like IT or sales. The study found that experience "in one additional functional area improved a person's odds of becoming a senior executive as much as three years of experience."[5] The findings also support the value in lateral career moves as part of moving along the corporate ladder, which may be important to you if your goal is to move into another department.

In your efforts to do the *right type of work* to boost your career, a little variety goes a long way. When you bring in the relationship view of our working reality, it makes sense that having experience in a range of skillsets means that you can better help any effort and impact more people.

ZERO IN ON PROJECTS THAT ARE VALUED

The best way to get recognized and build your career is to lead meaningful projects. We spoke with many successful professionals in a variety of fields to find out what they did that helped them get where they are today. We took the best ideas that are proven to make a difference and created a whole chapter of sample projects you can lead. Each of the eighteen projects in chapter 3, "Project Ideas to Spark Your Ignition," includes a rundown of what it's all about, including the benefits, examples of when it's a smart choice, the work required on your end, and more.

After we cover the basics of identifying the right type of work, we'll help you put this knowledge into action. We'll tell you how to create powerful narratives about your accomplishments that fix positive impressions in place—no matter what happened along the way. Then, as you approach your new stratum—your goal—and are in that critical moment when you could either fall back into the same old or achieve the outcome you want, we'll help you align with the big picture. Because companies are complex, multifaceted, and strategic, you need to know how to get in sync with what the next level up requires.

By applying the advice in this book, you can propel your career into the stratum you crave to be in. This is because what you do depends entirely on where you put your focus. As we go, these key areas will become progressively clearer. While getting to the next level is one thing, getting to your ultimate destination is another. We have designed this journey so that you can apply it over and over again as you navigate your career.

Collectively, your efforts and successes will build on each other until you have not only reached your destination but are thriving in it, excelling in it, and you are ready for yet another boost. This book is a guide to getting there—wherever that may be—every time you wish to launch again.

1

Build Your Platform for Takeoff

BOOSTING YOUR CAREER CAN ONLY HAPPEN WHEN you know how to set yourself up for success. The biggest challenge we see is that young and seasoned professionals alike jump into their first job or a new position, get working, and focus on that instead of on building their career. You get a job, which comes with a job description. Then you get assignments from your supervisor or manager. You do what you're told to do, work hard, turn in your work, and move on to the next assignment. But this is job maintenance—not career boosting.

If you want your accomplishments to be noticed, if you want to do great work and be celebrated for it, if you want to take one success and leverage it into the next, know this: it isn't chance that makes people successful. It's strategy. But unless you have an especially astute supervisor or mentor who helps you, no one will teach you what really matters in the workplace. Don't be left trying to figure it all out yourself—even the bright intuitions that help you along need to be informed and honed.

There are many components that determine whether or not you will make a meaningful impact. All of them depend on knowing what projects to focus on, what to throw your efforts into, and how to go about accomplishing important feats. So build a platform to stand on by erecting the four pillars offered in this chapter. From there, you will have the stability to launch yourself, your ideas, your projects, and your ambitions. You can aim high, definitely, but first establish the ground beneath you by knowing what's important to focus on and cultivate.

PILLAR #1: MULTIPLE BOSSES BRING MORE OPPORTUNITY

Boosting your career into orbit requires attention and approval from the players who matter most to your advancement. All of them. Because the truth is that in an organization, you have more than one real boss. Don't rely on the organizational hierarchy chart to determine who these people are, because many important influencers will not be in your direct chain of higher-ups. There are many people whose opinions matter to your success—all in different ways—and you need to get clear about who they are, how you can align your desires with theirs, and what roles they can play to aid your efforts.

It's a reality in today's workplace that the corporate ladder has turned into the corporate lattice. Employees once aimed to climb straight up to the top; now you need to navigate a structure with multiple pathways that lead across to other departments or to new roles requiring different skills or to opportunities elsewhere. So, to determine who you really, truly work for, don't look up—look everywhere.

Your Manager Is a Gateway

Let's get closer to the truth about success: not much can happen for you without your manager on your side. This person assigns you projects, approves your requests to lead new projects, confirms your successes, and encourages you to perform ever better. Your direct supervisor has the greatest pull when it comes to promotions and salary increases. That's why, in general, your professional life will most likely launch into the next stratum when he is behind your efforts. This person has a lot of power over your success, which makes him the most important boss to align yourself with.

Faced with the daily ups and downs, headache assignments, rote activities, or demanding due dates, it's easy to first blame your manager as the source of a problem. Inwardly, you can start to view him as a taskmaster when the inbox becomes flooded with requests, or a micromanager when he checks in about a project, or a deadline chaser during all those planning meetings. If you can't find some merit and only see your manager in that singular way, then you are going to stay on the ground.

Any supervisor's own success is measured by the accomplishments of his direct reports. So to boost your career the fastest, find ways to make him look good. Because when he feels good about your work, he'll share it with *his* boss, who might share it with the entire management team as an example. That is the quickest way to make an impact that travels throughout the organization. Whether you report to a board, a founding partner, a committee, a team lead, or within an elaborate chain of command, boosting the person who recommends your advancement boosts you every time. Once you learn how to make your supervisor look good, you can look around and target more people who will benefit from your efforts.

Boost Your Colleagues, So They Boost You

Yes, your peers have power over your career. Surprised? They may be the people in the cubicles next to you, the ones you go out to lunch with, and the people you share your thoughts, ideas, and also gripes with. They may represent another team across a meeting table, share your taste in music, or simply be the dudes who bring in the homemade cookies. Even though they are at your same level in the hierarchy or are possibly in a different branch of the company—especially if you work in a relatively flat organization or in a holocracy system—it is absolutely in your best interest to win the backing of your colleagues and peers.

This isn't about being fake and buttering them up just to make them like you. But here's a warning flag: if your projects or ideas or grumblings have a negative impact on them, it will result in negative attention. The last thing you want is for them to speak down about your attitude, your personality, or your work. And when you need them in the future for your big launch, they won't be there if you've burned bridges.

If you have the mindset that your colleagues are among your many bosses, you will work for their benefit. This is the absolute best way to regard colleagues, because when you benefit them, they will benefit you. Regard them as both bolsters for your reputation and boosters for your successes. You can easily and naturally become a leader by improving situations for your peers, so keep their needs in the forefront of your mind.

Leverage the Consensus of a Management Team

A nervous feeling in the pit of your stomach is common when around members of the senior management team. Because you sense—accurately—that what executives think of you matters. Their seniority means their opinions carry more weight.

Management teams come together to discuss promotions, problems, best-case scenarios, and new opportunities and to give one another feedback. In the same way that you benefit from your colleagues' approval, so does your supervisor. Just because your boss is the one to tell you about a promotion, don't think the decision is made alone. It's tough, if not impossible, to promote a person the team doesn't approve of collectively. Most senior leaders readily speak their minds when it comes to anyone who stands out, whether in good or bad ways. So think of the management or executive team as a consensual power that you want on your side. Because if they notice you and they think highly of you, your efforts to launch will be propelled forward by them, possibly reaching greater heights than you could imagine.

So when you look at who you work for, include the people managing other teams. They all have many needs and goals, both individual and shared, which gives you a lot of opportunity to provide support. Keeping this big picture of a company's collective efforts in mind will help you stand apart as someone who can help all the gears turn. This helps your value and contributions to be recognized by everyone on the management team—support that your supervisor will keep funneling directly to you.

Get Direct Reports to Speak Up in All the Right Ways

Your reports work with you closely. They see and talk about how you respond to opportunities and setbacks and how you approach a challenge. Their opinions shape your reputation more than you realize, and they carry a lot of clout. If you are a smart, supportive, results-oriented, genuine human being—people will know. If you are a disengaged, lazy, self-absorbed, or dictatorial boss—people will know even sooner. Reports share their feelings about you, if not blatantly, then through subtleties that are not lost on your coworkers or manager.

When preparing to boost your career, realize that the ways you manage your reports affect your reputation and your success within the company. You can use their feedback to take responsibility for becoming a more effective manager, which fuels the successes your team needs to set you on your way.

It is often said that employees are reflections of their managers, so if your reports are mediocre, it makes you look like a mediocre leader. Their performance matters. If your group hasn't done anything noteworthy lately or your reports are regularly missing quotas or deadlines or are falling short of goals—for whatever reason—you look like the dolt. But if coworkers think of your team as committed, competent, impactful producers, as their leader you are celebrated as the mastermind behind their successes. So go out of your way to lead them in troubleshooting and problem-solving. Give full support to great ideas, which includes lending your own skills and knowledge, making resources available, and helping them juggle their priorities and workloads.

Adopt the mindset that a win for your reports is also a personal win for you. As a leader, your job is to bring out the best in your people and help develop and upgrade their strengths. Definitely think about how their involvement will gain them positive attention in your company. This will serve your reputation as a leader well and make a great contribution to your own launch.

A Happy Client Is the Greatest Sign of Success

If you spend a lot of time working directly with clients or customers—such as in a high-touch service business like consulting, advertising, or social marketing—there's a good chance they are indeed one of your real bosses. Think about where your income is coming from: who is ultimately paying for your services? Keeping clients happy, and therefore loyal, will make your supervisor and other leaders even happier.

When customers aren't pleased with how a company does business, they spread complaints like wildfire. And when they're happy, the great news is that they also let the world know it. Through social media, online reviews, and good old word of mouth, it's easy to get feedback. This demands that companies and their employees stay accountable: negative feedback makes it hard to bring in new business or get referrals; positive feedback does the opposite—it boosts your entire effort into expansion. So fulfill the needs of your clients by working diligently for them.

Even if you don't work directly with clients, know that your job depends on their happiness. They want a quality product, so provide one. They want great service, so be sure client-facing colleagues have what they need. They want to feel good about the company they partner with, so make efforts to get involved in things like environmentally friendly practices, hiring veterans, diversity, and especially social responsibility. They want companies to be transparent, behave ethically, and not succumb to corporate greed. So work to give them whatever they need to feel good about hiring your services or buying your product.

Be aware: sometimes the client's power as a boss is magnified. If your company is losing market share on a certain product, or you're trying to bounce back after negative attention, making clients happy will become top priority. Keep an eye out for those times, because if you can find ways to win additional business from current clients or find ways to appeal to new ones, you'll be soaring in no time.

Use the Power of HR

You may not work with the human resources department very often, but it's an undeniable fact that you always work for them. While HR's role varies from company to company, its opinions matters. It's best to have HR staffers on your side because they consulted on the current roles everyone has, and they will consult on what roles and which people stay crucial to success—and which can be let go. HR employees know where the movement is happening, what's being restructured, or the changes a department is in the midst of getting approved. And they have the most power over employee continuity and changeover when a company is facing a merger or acquisition.

Be sure your HR team would recommend you, regardless of the situation or the direction you aim to launch into. Stay on HR's radar, as their approval is among the most powerful. The best way to do this is casually, by stopping in and saying hi, having coffee together, and syncing up. Fill the team in a little on the projects you're working on, share your goals, and, if appropriate to their role, ask for their input. When the HR staff not only have you in mind but also think of you highly at the top of their mind, you're standing exactly where you need to be to accurately launch.

Whose Support Matters?

You have the desire to get somewhere, to grow, to expand, to be valued. Sometimes we know exactly where we want to end up, and sometimes we only discover that along the way as we pursue success. Either way, you need to identify whose support matters. We've given you some ideas for who they might be; now it's your turn to get specific. List their names. Describe their roles in the company you work for, in your industry, among your client base, or within your service sector. Clarify how their support might help you. Then comes the most important part: identify how you can work for each of them. Here are some examples:

- If you want to excel in your current role, get clear about the things that are most important to your "boss" and do them in an A+ fashion.
- If you're interested in moving into operations, think about how processes that worked at other jobs can improve decisions made in your company.
- If you want a global opportunity, do some research, take global management courses, and then consider how something your team does might help a team working abroad.
- If you think marketing might be a good fit for you, meet with a savvy marketing mentor first. Then approach someone on that team and share some ideas for how your department can better support their efforts. Making this initial connection will establish her as a new boss who may eventually support a lateral move.

Taking this type of action will get you noticed by the right people and get them thinking about you and your skills in new, fresh, and exciting ways.

PILLAR #2: SIMPLICITY MAKES THE RIGHT KIND OF WAVES

Don't make the mistake of thinking work that makes an impact must be time consuming and complicated. Up until now, you may have assumed that the harder you work on something, the more successful you will be. But if you're working on the things that don't matter to your boss, you could simply be digging a bigger hole to stagnate in rather than building the platform for your launch.

That's why you need to get rid of the idea that bigger is better. Just erase it. Because the ideas that make the most meaningful impacts are the simplest. For example, on Monday mornings before work, at 7:30 a.m. in a nearby coffee shop, get your group together to talk about innovation. As they come off the weekend, before the work day begins, everyone's minds will be fresh. It's a small idea, but it gathers momentum toward creative thinking and problem-solving. It could have big effects: on how the team approaches challenges; on coming up with new solutions to customer needs; on getting processes out of their habitual groove so they stay flexible and responsive; and on thinking outside the box throughout the week in a variety of tasks. Innovation can become a genuine part of the group's momentum and a key to the group's success—all of which boosts you. See how initiating something simple can have serious results? It can even create a cultural shift.

When looking for opportunities to do work that makes a meaningful impact, you don't need to set out to create the next big thing. All companies have limited time and resources; all people have limited time and resources. Your time has measurable value, and you have a budget. So consider your company's return on a project, and keep it simple. Here are guidelines for choosing opportunities to pursue that will help you keep things unpretentious, doable, and realistic—and will therefore demonstrate that you get things done.

Play to Your Strengths

We live in a culture that embraces self-improvement and encourages us to develop into the most accomplished people we can be. Amidst all this striving to do more and be more, it's easy to forget the things you're pretty darn good at already. You should think about your skills and talents as the strongest muscles in your body. When you flex those muscles, you set yourself up for much better results. If you needed to lift forty pounds, would you rather bench press it or use your pinky toe? When you play to your strengths, you create a personal brand and naturally differentiate yourself from others.

Don't get tripped up by thinking that doing something that's inherently easy for you will make your work obsolete. Don't be tempted to try and impress anyone with complex efforts. Don't reach outside the skillset you already have and are known for. Here are two reasons why.

First, your clients, colleagues, and supervisors view your work through their own lenses of strengths and weaknesses. What comes so quickly and easily to you might not happen like that for others. The task that you see as a no-brainer could be a stress producer for your team or company or entrepreneurial venture. Say that, for you, data takes minutes to analyze and draw meaning—that could very well be a stroke of genius to them. Think about it. If it was actually that easy for everyone to do, someone else would've already reached those conclusions. Keep this in mind if you're tense about proposing a project that seems so easy and obvious that you wonder if it will have any impact at all. The reality is, it could make a huge difference to people who don't have your strengths.

Second, you're on the clock when you're doing impact work, whether you work an hourly, contract, or salaried job. You don't have all day to snail crawl your way to making a difference. Time is money—if not your own money, then someone else's. When you play to your strengths you'll work more efficiently and can power through your task list, which makes your efforts that much more impressive.

So choose or adapt projects that flex your strongest, most impressive muscles. If you're a great writer, incorporate written communication into your projects. If you're excellent at spotting trends, use it and showcase your predictive ability. If you can wield the arts of persuasion and win people over with a cool and breezy demeanor, apply those skills to finding new clients. If social networking is your forte, build your impact projects around using it to attract new business or create internal camaraderie.

By playing to your strengths, the work feels easier and you won't be reaching out of your element—even if you're doing something new. You are also more likely to get great results, which will build the confidence and self-esteem that will keep you aiming high.

Your Strongest Muscles at Work

It's smart to write down your natural strengths and talents and add to the list as you develop new ones. This is because when your strengths are top of mind, you can call on these aptitudes to help you with your impact projects so that they are simple and low stress.

Do you know what you're good at? When you consider your strengths, you might have a different perspective than your colleagues, family members, or friends. You may be too humble, suffer from self-doubt, or only have a vague sense, so asking around will help.

- Take a moment to think about what you excel at and write down at least three of your strengths in business. Be careful not to simply repeat compliments you've been given. Do your own soul searching. If strengths don't jump into mind, think about winning situations you've had a part in: What did you bring to the picture? Stick with this inquiry, and arrive at some powerful answers. This is incredibly important for the self-awareness that this book builds on.

- Next, ask close friends, family members, mentors, or trusted colleagues what they believe you're good at. You can say you're doing a professional development project and need input from people who know you well. Write down what they tell you.

- How did the answers compare? Most people hear things from others that they didn't recognize on their own. It can be an eye-opening experience and one that helps you better play to your strengths in the future.

Many companies make exercises like this one a part of their performance review process. You can find them online, and I recommend Gallup's *StrengthsFinder 2.0* as a good self-evaluating tool. It's known to point out less obvious skills, like your natural propensity to include others, your love for learning new things, or your ability to quickly connect with strangers. This information can give you a fresh perspective to consider. And the more strengths you can identify, the wider your field of opportunity becomes. So play the game well, play it straight, play it strong, and use your best muscles to give your career that boost.

Less Truly Is More. Seriously.

Too often, good ideas transform into something overly complicated—which makes them no longer viable. I've seen this happen so many times over the years working with pharmaceutical products. Companies would spend a lot of money on marketing, advertising, celebrity endorsements, online efforts, and direct mail. But even with all these expensive and complex promotional efforts, sales remained flat or even behind quota and losing market share. These companies had large budgets and were trying so many approaches, but nothing was working.

In situations like this, the best move is to take a fresh look and come up with new, simple solutions. It takes brainstorming and research and a willingness to question the status quo. It turned out that pharmaceutical customers weren't responding to traditional marketing tactics because the messages were coming from the wrong people. We were at the beginning of the peer-to-peer marketing movement. With the rise of social media, consumers were not persuaded by traditional advertising because they were starting to buy products and services based on online testimony and reviews. Once I saw this, I could accurately attribute disappointing sales to a less effective communication strategy and work with these companies to simplify their marketing into a single focus: high-profile, respected people speaking to their peers.

In case you don't believe me, here are four powerful ways that less turns out to be more.

Less Risk to Time and Money
When you have a short timeline and keep resources small, your project is less of a gamble for your reputation, your career, and your company. So much is at stake if you spend years working on something and invest thousands—or even millions—of dollars in resources and manpower. If you get bad results, you may find yourself in a painful position. On the flip side, when you just spend a few half days working on something, or a series of weeknights after work, getting negative results isn't a very big deal. Nothing gained, but nothing lost. Remember, Edison failed two thousand times working on the filament before he discovered the light bulb. Apply the power of persistence, one simple project at a time.

Fewer Things Can Go Wrong
A vast array of moving parts is hard to control. A cascade of effects is inevitable, whether positive or negative. When things go wrong in one place, those problems can create other problems, which—

you guessed it—create even more problems. Small projects are manageable, and there are fewer opportunities for trouble. It's also easier to foresee potential problems and address them before they get big enough to cause a setback. So give yourself something reasonable to manage.

Less Risk Socially and Politically

When you make bold choices or find clever solutions to old problems, you need to consider who you might upset. Most people dislike change, and your ideas could cause discomfort or even opposition, especially if you're new to the team. Office politics can be such a drag, but they are a very real part of your working environment. It's in your best interest to get a better sense of the connections that affect workplace dynamics. Mechele has a great way of looking at this conundrum. She calls them "Tarzan chains," which are the strong links between individuals that are hidden in the jungle of day-to-day work. Tarzan chains can be hard to see and can be connections you would never expect, like the colleague who is family friends with a powerful client. Or the fact that you went to school with the COO's youngest sister. Or your boss plays golf on weekends with your ad agency VP. It's smart to understand these chains well before you try to shake things up with an epic demonstration of muscle. Smaller projects have less chance of throwing the jungle into chaos and turning people against you.

Less Noticeable If It Fails

You don't want to hide outcomes that don't meet expectations, but you don't want to broadcast them either. Smaller projects are much better at flying under the radar, especially when they're still in progress. Colleagues may hear about the project, but if they aren't directly involved, it's just a blip on the radar. If nothing notable happens, it's likely people quickly will have forgotten the project ever existed on your to-do list.

Think about small, highly noticeable projects as low-hanging fruit. If you know you can drive an under-quota product so it meets its estimated annual forecast, great. But even solving an office nuisance can bring you accolades. Look for opportunities that have a high chance for success without a large investment. Being able to spot low-hanging fruit is paramount to your success, because you will achieve greater outcomes through minimal work.

Eliminating an Irritant Spikes Happiness

Sometimes the best thing you can do isn't creating something new—it's getting rid of something people dislike. There has been a vast amount of research done on the psychology behind what makes people happy. We tend to think that having *more* drives happiness—more money, more material possessions, bigger houses, the newest technology, the latest model car. But researchers have found that people experience greater spikes in happiness when they remove unwanted tasks from their to-do lists, such as housekeeping, supermarket shopping, check writing, yard work, or taxes.[6] While getting help with disagreeable tasks isn't too difficult or expensive, we mistakenly focus on the urge to acquire bigger or better things. When we get some discretionary income, we think it's smarter to buy something new instead of paying to get rid of something we dislike, like housework. Why? Because it's feels like a less stressful change to keep doing the mildly irritating but familiar things we're already doing. In the moment, it seems quicker and easier than creating a long-term solution to end the problem for good. We are creatures of habit, often to a fault. That's why we continuously suffer through things that annoy us.

Apply these research findings to the professional world, and use them to your advantage when thinking about work that will have a meaningful impact. Eliminating an irritant can cause waves of happiness in the office. If you can identify something that irks your boss, coworkers, or clients on a regular basis and figure out how to fix it, you're going to be thanked profusely. Here are simple things you could do to thrill your colleagues.

- Decrease the number of long and drawn-out meetings by establishing a shorter format of thirty-minute standups that have pre-established agendas.
- Shorten the automated message that plays every time someone calls the office. Change the hold music.
- Buy a can of WD-40 and silence those squeaky hinged doors and cabinets all over the office, change the dead lightbulbs, and look up how to fix the jam in the fax machine. Get a screwdriver and tighten the door handles and doorknob plates that flap every time you open the office doors. It's not your job, but it is your community stressor, and it makes the office feel professional, elegant, and pain-in-the-neck free.
- Put a cell-phone collection basket at the door to the meeting room to eliminate distracting rings and inattention.
- Talk to the finance department about simplifying the expense approval process so managers only need to sign off on purchases above a certain amount.
- Conduct a "speak softly" awareness campaign to enhance concentration in open office settings.

Changes like these may seem small, but they feel like significant improvements. You know those electronic buzzing sounds you don't notice until they're silenced? People don't realize how annoying something truly was until it goes away. The more people you can impact by eliminating an irritant, the better. This is often one of the easiest ways to get noticed by a lot of people, all the way up to the C-suite.

So keep an eye out for anything particularly exasperating at your job that could be changed. Leaders are especially pleased when employees spot workplace disturbances and get rid of them. And most professional people we know are irritated by anything that wastes their time, irritates their senses, feels redundant, or adds little value. As you think about potential projects, focus on those issues.

Do you see how you don't need to create a new Expedia, set up a better Uber, or have a life-changing idea to make a difference? Ideas that don't seem revolutionary at all sometimes have surprising impact. Like Starbucks' pumpkin spice latte, a.k.a. the PSL, or McDonald's all-day breakfast. The employees at those companies thought of a deft, albeit simple, idea that garnered a cult following. Not only did their ideas catch fire and catapult sales, they impacted the companies overall, helping them gain an even greater competitive advantage. Even organizing a company blood drive is a simple idea and a truly life-changing good deed. It has impact on many levels, both inside and outside your business, as employees rally to donate. This shows how keeping your efforts strong, simple, and user friendly can get results that people appreciate. Sometimes all it takes is a fresh perspective, a new idea, some flair, and a knack for disrupting business as usual in smart ways.

PILLAR #3: CHANGE KEEPS YOU DYNAMIC

It's commonly said that what people fear most are death and public speaking. But in my experience, this isn't true. Most people fear change more than anything else. By nature, people are creatures of habit. We like to go into the office every day and know where our desk is, how the coffee machine works, who the security people are at the building entrance, and on what holidays we get paid time off. We like this type of certainty because it's easy and comfortable. We know what to expect, and our brains can relax instead of constantly gearing up for new situations that could call for different behaviors.

Although there is comfort in routine, organizations just don't stay the same for long. Clients' and customers' needs change, the competition evolves, employees come and go, and mergers or acquisitions happen. Sometimes the only thing you can count on is change. You might not know eventual outcomes, but change is inevitable; to boost your career, you need to embrace it by staying dynamic.

Get Used to Stretching Yourself

You can choose to cultivate one of two habits: keeping everything stagnant so you stay comfortable or becoming comfortable within an ever-changing environment. If you stay within your comfort zone, where everything is familiar and inactive, I can guarantee you'll stay the same too. Even if you rack your brain and come up with new, fresh, innovative ideas, you won't be able to follow through with them unless you know how to move on with change.

Fuel the dynamic mindset that creativity depends on by continuously refreshing your perspective on the world around you. It's essential that you get out, have new experiences, and do things like meeting people from other fields who could help you see your work from a different vantage point. Sometimes getting out of your comfort zone is as simple as getting out of your neighborhood. *Science* magazine did a study based on cell phone data and found it's possible to predict human movement patterns up to 93 percent of the time. Most people stick to the same small six-mile radius or less and visit the same locations at the same times of day. The same study found that even frequent travelers retain the same patterns, so even though crossing thousands of miles, they still stay in the same small radiuses.[7] They frequent the same restaurants, the same supermarket, and the same places to socialize. They take the same streets or form of transportation to work, and they walk the dog or exercise on the same route. With so many grooves of habit worn so deep, no wonder people rely on a mental autopilot to get through life. And they make it obvious why innovation feels hard.

You could easily be living in such a small bubble. By staying in it, you are limiting the number of new experiences you have and therefore eliminating the chance to have fresh reactions, even *aha!*

moments of insight. Without new people and their totally unique inputs, you can't get fueled up with ideas. You need to mix things up, because when you do something differently or go someplace new, your brain goes from autopilot to active. You notice your surroundings. You pay attention to what you're doing. You're engaged in the freshness of the present moment. Here are tips for getting outside of your comfort zone.

- Take a class and learn something you know nothing about, whether it's glass blowing, UX and digital strategy basics, digital advertising, cooking Thai food, or trying a new yoga style.
- Have a meal in a new restaurant and try eating a type of cuisine you've never had before.
- Say yes when a friend or coworker asks you to do something you would usually turn down.
- Attend a conference, go to a public lecture at a university or community house, or listen to a webinar that offers advice for another industry.
- Take the kids or dog to a new park.
- Go for a walk without a predetermined route or destination. Just see where your mood takes you. Your cell phone can always bring you back.
- Take a weekend trip to a new city. It doesn't have to be fancy or far away, just somewhere new to you.
- Call some new acquaintances and meet for dinner.
- Pick up a magazine you've never read or flip to a section of the newspaper you usually ignore. This will inspire you to think about new things.

By intentionally doing things differently, you can keep your mind sharp and ready to come up with new ideas. It's a new-you state of mind, always ready to embrace change, think differently, gain new perspectives, and, most of all, unleash your innovation.

Norms Point Out Where Change Is Needed

We can act a certain way just because that's always been the way we act. Long-established processes continue to be followed simply because they have always been that way. Even traditional business roles seem to be more based in habit than anything else. When you run across a norm like this, immediately begin to question it. Is it the best way to do this? Does it produce the results people assume it does? Who is it serving: customers, management, stakeholders, or legacy employees? Can it be accomplished more efficiently with new technology? A great way to make a meaningful impact in your company is to question these long-standing norms and explore opportunities for positive disruption or improvement.

One of my favorite "disrupters" is Howard Safir, former New York City fire commissioner and police commissioner. He often speaks to my MBA students at Fordham. Safir came up through the ranks as a police officer by caring deeply about his job and helping people. As fire commissioner, he noticed that because his team responded quickly to calls, they could address the fire but were paralyzed to help the victims. While waiting for paramedics to arrive, people would go into cardiac arrest and firefighters could only stand by and watch. One firefighter suggested that they become certified first-responders and be supplied with basic life-saving equipment. "After all," he said, "aren't we in the business of saving lives? Shouldn't we walk the talk?" Safir created a plan and budget for getting defibrillators and training firefighters on how to use them. Former mayor Rudy Giuliani recognized what an improvement this would deliver to the citizens of New York City, and he approved Safir's plan on the spot. As a bonus, firefighters were each paid more for expanding their skillset, but the increased pride they felt in their work was even more rewarding. Safir's ability to question long-standing norms led to an innovative idea that continues to save lives today.

Staying dynamic means getting out of pigeonholes. Dynamism and disruption absolutely go hand in hand. So doing things like taking courses outside your job description, such as graphic and software design, operations research, or cybersecurity, expresses your dynamism and prepares you for the flexible startup economy that is ahead. When Mechele took a digital marketing course to broaden her consulting reach, she learned things her traditional marketing MBA could never have imagined would someday be possible. She learned more ways to help her clients evaluate and address their app opportunities and potential. And, with a partner, she even launched an app called Partyology for stress-free party giving.

So keep it a core value to regularly rub off the rust in your skillset. This will keep you relevant. On a basic level, you'll keep up with a dynamic business environment, which will keep you employed. But you want more than this. Become someone who can learn quickly, make essential pivots, change directions as needed, and come up with ideas for embracing new directions. Be a change-agent and stay ahead of the curve. All the time.

PILLAR #4: IDEAS FOR INNOVATION ARE EVERYWHERE

Believe in yourself—your innovation skills are there. You just need the courage and stamina to bring them to the surface. Becoming more comfortable with change than with stagnation is the first step. Next, you need to get rid of worn-in, cliché assumptions about creativity and replace them with habits that stir up your thinking. Because the truth is, when you're alert to inspiration, ideas for new ways to do things are everywhere. It won't necessarily feel easy, but positive thinking eventually brings you the outcome you envision.

Borrow Old Ideas and Apply Them to Get New Results

It's really hard to innovate when you think you must come up with something that is 100 percent new in every way. That mentality is exactly why people get frustrated, give up, and let the status quo continue. Considering the number of ideas in the world today, nothing is ever completely original. What *is* original is how people combine existing ideas with new concepts. For example, a top-forty song could be inspired by both jazz and rock legends and have lyrics that describe a current event. A designer's new fashion collection could riff off a popular style from twenty years ago and mesh it with elements from India. In innovations like these, it can be impossible to pinpoint all the different sources of inspiration because the finished product has transformed into something original. In the workplace, you can borrow ideas from anywhere. Here are a few places.

Stay Alert to Competitor Innovation

Yes, you could research your competitors for ideas, but that is just a tiny fraction of the inspiration available to you. If your competitors are doing something inventive, you need to pay attention but also push yourself beyond safe convention. It is essential to keep a close eye on competitive innovations and then challenge yourself to rework or improve upon them and forge new territory. Think Steve Jobs . . . Aside from competitors, there is a lot of inspiration available from improbable sources.

Adapt from Other Industries

Other industries may be applying ideas to a totally different product, but they offer solutions and practices you can adapt and use in your domain. In the book *Not Invented Here*, authors Ramon Vullings and Marc Heleven get to the heart of this innovation opportunity when they write, "Cross-industry innovation is a clever way to jump-start your innovation efforts by drawing analogies and transferring approaches between contexts, beyond the borders of your own industry, sector, area, or domain."[8] Here are examples of this kind of melding and inspirational hacking.

- BMW's iDrive system was inspired by a video console.

- The Waffle shoe was inspired by a waffle iron used by founder Bill Bowerman's wife.
- The Worx automatic screwdriver was inspired by a revolver gun—drill bits can be loaded like bullets.
- Doug Dietz of GE Healthcare redesigned CT-scan rooms to be more like game parks so children would feel less afraid.
- Sushi restaurants use airport-style conveyor belts to provide diners a wide range of fresh dishes.

Ideas like these are not earth shattering—far from it. They are practical adaptions and solutions that rejigger habits and routines to bring new contexts. Madanmohan Rao, research director at YourStory Media, said, "What can a restaurant learn from an airport, a car manufacturer from the games industry, a hospital from a hotel or theme park, or a chemical company from a festival organizer? . . . The key is to go beyond 'copy and paste' to 'adapt and paste,' via enrichment, customization, modification, blending, and fusion."[9] If something pops into your head, write it down, keep a list in your phone, and begin to live with an innovative mindset.

Bring Two Tried-and-True Things Together
Combining unlikely elements is a great way to come up with something revolutionary. Think how Jeff Bezos has created an online empire by combining a department store with home delivery. Amazon now even delivers food to your home or business and is test marketing same-day delivery—in some cases by drone!

Mary Kay Ash also did this in 1963 when she launched a beauty company with a direct-selling model. This sales model had been around for years, but not for beauty products. Her idea took off because customers loved buying beauty products from home, especially from women they already knew. Beauty consultant salespeople loved the flexible part-time schedule and a direct sales job that had women as the target market. Ash's idea of selling makeup in home through demonstrations given by friends and neighbors was unconventional at that time. Her idea serves as the genesis for today's popular Botox parties and all of the many products now marketed through at-home get-togethers, like women's fashion, gift basket-making, baking and food preparation products, even sex toy and intimacy products.

Zip Drug is another company that combined two great ideas—delivery service and prescriptions. Although you could buy just about anything online, including fresh groceries delivered from local stores, there were few options for delivering prescriptions to your door within an hour. Zip Drug is filling that need by allowing customers to place orders through a smartphone app.

Pilfer Concepts That Underlie Other Innovations

Riffing off others' styles or inventions is what makes for classier fashion, more usable technology, and more efficient solutions to daily living.

There is a great book about drawing inspiration from others called *Steal Like an Artist: 10 Things Nobody Told You About Being Creative* by Austin Kleon. In this book, Kleon explains how copying others' ideas is a natural thing people do from childhood, but there is a right way and a wrong way to do it. "Don't just steal the style, steal the thinking behind the style," says Kleon. "You don't want to look like your heroes. You want to see like them."[10]

Kleon emphasizes that you are the sum of all your influences—a mashup of what you choose to let into your life. This is especially useful in business, because the philosophy behind a given finished product may have solved problems you also face. Seeing how others innovate is the best part to borrow from because their result is the best current resolution to a market dilemma. You could do even better. Once they demonstrate the pure value of the product or service, you can always innovate further to bring customers the best option out there.

> ### Train Yourself to See Innovation Everywhere
>
> Keep track of good ideas you see. You might want to borrow them later, but more importantly the simple act of appreciating innovation when you see it will exercise your own muscles. Kleon recommends jotting them all down in one place.[11] So, as you live your freshly inspired life, out of the box, pay attention to anything that grabs you as a good idea and be ready to whip out a pocket notebook. As you write down the idea, also ask yourself: *What makes this a good idea?*
>
> - Does it solve a clear problem?
> - Has it nailed a product's positioning and branding advantage?
> - Does it surprise you?
> - Is it a quirky, unique, and original play on a familiar thing?
> - Have they applied elements from various industries?
> - Is it an old product or service, repackaged for a new market segment?
>
> As you think about projects that could make an impact, this list could serve as a source of inspiration. And by identifying the thinking behind the concept, you can stir your own brainstorms and widen your reach so that you are drawing ideas from everywhere.

Support Other People's Ideas

The best idea in the room won't always be your own. And that's okay—in fact, that's great. Inspiring leaders support an innovative environment where ideas can grow and thrive. When your colleagues share ideas, be the person in the room to speak up and compliment their thinking. Share what you like about the idea. Offer to meet later to brainstorm further. Don't do it as a favor—do it because you're genuinely interested in helping to come up with the next great thing, be it a product, service, process tweak, marketing angle, design flair, usability improvement, or delivery platform.

Be the kind of colleague others want to have in their close groups. Creativity expert and author Pamela Meyer says that when you're supportive of your coworkers' ideas and try to build on them, people see you as an "energizer"—someone who makes them feel positive about themselves and their ideas. That's a great quality to make part of your personal brand. In Meyer's book *From Workplace to Playspace*, she says that energizers also happen to be the highest performers and that people actively seek out help from energizers when they have a new idea or project.[12] Her findings conclude energizers get more opportunities to work on important projects and collaborate more with higher-ups than their colleagues. When given the choice, of course we all want to work with people who are helpful and make us feel good. Know that when you help other people, you also help yourself. So make it a personal goal to become "the" energizer.

You can spark this kind of collaborative innovation-thinking by encouraging your team to meet weekly in a quiet environment to share innovative ideas they have noted. Even if the ideas don't feel applicable, they may make for great fodder for the group's brainstorms. They unleash creativity. That's the kind of thinking that gave birth to the Airbnb concept and the self-serve frozen yogurt places where you can get exactly what you want, even if you didn't know you wanted it. We all love ideas like those.

The secret to innovation that you can apply across all your efforts to boost your career is this: it is a state of mind. It can be cultivated, honed, inspired, and regularly fed so that your creative thinking grows. This dynamic mental state can be applied to anything and everything, one meaningful project at a time, as you take aim and launch toward wherever you want to go.

MOMENTUM-BUILDING STRATEGIES

Instead of toiling away—putting blood, sweat, and tears into your work—this chapter has shown you how to work smart and to focus your activity on things that really matter. Keep these four pillars top of mind, and you'll have a stable platform for your launch toward your career goal. Here are the key strategies that will do this.

- The more people you serve through your efforts, the wider your base of opportunity becomes.
- Keep things simple by using your strongest muscles, minimizing risk, and making everyone happier by finding solutions to pesky problems.
- Become a change agent by expanding your lifestyle to include new, fresh, and stimulating experiences.
- Make innovation a habit of mind that you can apply to any endeavor.

2

Fuel Up with the Support You Need

NO ENDEAVOR GETS OFF THE GROUND WITHOUT fuel. This may have happened to you: you've got an idea and you're totally enthused about it. Say you see a totally new market for your product and have dreamed up all kinds of ways to reach it. If you were a company of one, your own enthusiasm may be all the fuel you need to spark ignition, launch, and enter a new orbit in your career. But it's more likely that you have investors, or a board, or a supervisor, or a whole arrangement of higher-ups. You have team members you need to recruit, vendors offering services you need, clients needing to be onboarded. And suddenly you're being asked endless questions that stall progress. You're getting requests for reports, proposals, projections, cost estimates, and timelines. Everyone wants to feel reassured. They want their concerns addressed, and someone always seems to have yet another concern. A devil's advocate might arise, a worst-case scenario posed that stops you short. Suddenly your overnight stroke of genius is burdened by everyone's individual point of view.

So are you going to win their support? Are you going to get the fuel you need to get your project off the ground? If you were to interview a wide range of high-stratum businesspeople and leaders, as we did, and ask them to share their secrets about what it takes to make the most significant impacts—the ones that have boosted their careers—you would hear a whole lot about relationships. Everyone we spoke with talked about how vital interpersonal dynamics are to success. What do the best leaders have in common? They strive to cultivate positive emotional connections.

A surprising number of people we interviewed take it a step further. They confided that their secret success propellant is not just positive relationships—it's actively helping others. This is their core philosophy: that to make an impact, you must *want* to help others and make them look good. What makes projects *meaningful* is that they help the people around you. By consistently being available and even eager to help, you can build a stellar reputation as the quick-fix guy, the go-to girl, the experienced advisor, the idea-infuser, the exciter, or the person who takes an idea and runs with it. Reputations like those offer the support you need for your launch. Whether client, superior, or newbie intern, this is what's needed to win support and respect for anything you do. This is the very fuel that gets you where you want to go.

Just as there are several stages in a career, many types of efforts, a whole lot of projects, and a plethora of people to work with, there are also different types of fuel that propel you in different circumstances. That's why we're sharing seven kinds of propellants that each give you the support you need, when you need it. In chapter 1, we covered the multiple "real bosses" at your job, from supervisors to colleagues to customers. Keep all these people in mind as you find ways to apply the relationship advice in this chapter. Because you aren't working in a static environment, situations change rapidly, and you can't know which relationships will be important in the future. The best thing you can do is make sure you're thinking about everyone.

PROPELLANT #1: THE PERSON YOU HELP HELPS YOU

If you want people to help you, help them first. Going out of your way to do things for people will motivate them to help you when you need it. But here's the fine art of paying it forward: when you help someone out, don't expect anything in return. People know when your heart and mind are in the right place.

People can also tell when you're out for personal gain. Doing a favor to get a favor doesn't make for a good business relationship. Some leaders do think of the people in their midst as being nothing more than resources. But they're the ones who will linger midair or even fall away when they hit a new atmosphere. Because thinking that way is disingenuous, it acts against making meaningful impacts.

Instead, be a trusted leader. If you are, no matter what level you're currently working on, the people around you will fuel you with the support you need when you need it. Whether you have proactively decided to help someone or they asked you directly to help, be genuinely interested in achieving their goal. This is an essential value proposition that underlies good business practices and is the unspoken golden rule of business. As the brilliant scientist Albert Einstein said, "Try not to become a [person] of success, but rather try to become a [person] of value."

This operates through the paradox of happiness. Many studies have shown that doing something for other people is actually more rewarding, and makes you feel happier, than doing something nice for yourself. So when you support others' work and they turn around to support yours, everyone feels really good in the process. Call it workplace karma, servant leadership, or just being a good person, this true desire to help others is something you can always feel happy about.

PROPELLANT #2: MAKE YOURSELF VALUABLE TO EVERYONE

It's easy to be valuable to coworkers within your own department. You talk with those people every day, your work may benefit them directly, and they repeatedly see the good you're doing. You offer value just by showing up and doing your regular job in a five-star manner. It can seem harder to be valuable across departments, divisions, and levels—even companies and industries—but that's how you make a big impact. It increases your visibility, gains recognition, and builds a reputation. This is important, because your competitor could easily be your next partner.

Heather Hahn has a knack for building relationships with coworkers. Her approach is based on a very simple theory: "Be nice to everyone so no one has anything bad to say about you." When Heather worked as an event coordinator for Legoland, she won 2012 Employee of the Year, an honor given to one person in one thousand. To choose the winner, all the Legoland VPs get together in one room and talk about which employee deserves to win the award based on their impact. When Heather's name was brought up, all the VPs not only knew who she was but could also think of a time when Heather had worked with them individually to further their goals, eliminate wasted time, or help their departments in memorable ways. She wasn't chasing personal glory—she won the award by offering goal-related assistance to different departments.

When Heather's name was announced as the award winner at the company banquet, she was initially shocked. Yet when she looked around the room, she realized she knew just about everybody who was applauding. From the newest hire to the senior muckety mucks, from the receptionists to the IT techs, she had taken the time to get to know all her coworkers—and it was noticed.

This wasn't the first time Heather's ability to build cross-departmental relationships had helped her. Before working at Legoland, Heather was the promotions and entertainment manager for Tampa Bay's hockey team, the Lightning. In this role, she had many real bosses because she worked directly with a variety of people, both inside and outside the company. She worked with the group tickets department to make sure their customers got special recognition. She became ingrained in the community by organizing the team's involvement in parades and ideas like dyeing the city river "Lightning" blue. Heather was rarely at her desk, as she was mostly out and about meeting with people, in person. Her work affected so many colleagues and clients that when the hockey team marketing department went through a massive layoff, Heather was one of the only people who wasn't let go. "I made myself valuable for too many departments," she said, reflecting on her retention. "They would have missed me too much."[13]

Having these strong relationships with colleagues in other sectors of your organization is essential for a variety of reasons. It deepens your understanding of the business and what you can do, within your role, to make an impact. People will open up to you about what challenges their department is facing, and you then come to understand how all the gears turn. This gives you the background you need to perceive opportunities for solutions, improvements, innovation, and other ways to help.

Interdepartmental and multilevel relationships can also help you become aware of different areas in which your skills and strengths can be useful, which may spark an interest that launches you in a new direction. Our Spanish-fluent friend Maida Chicon volunteers at the Fresh Air Fund, a nonprofit that takes kids out of the inner city for country vacation breaks. When she began volunteering by helping families fill out the necessary paperwork, she didn't foresee she would be called upon by other departments. They valued her MBA knowledge and corporate-honed talents, and soon she was helping with their internship program and cultivating relationships with new donors. If you decide you do want to learn more about another role or department, it helps to know people already embedded in it. They can help you assess whether you might want to be part of that team someday. Because once you are established as a valuable and trusted colleague, it's easier to pursue opportunities anywhere in your organization.

PROPELLANT #3: POSITIVE CONNECTIONS YIELD POSITIVE RESULTS

Winning awards and surviving a surprise round of layoffs are the constructive results of making an impact, but they were never Heather Hahn's specific goals. Her intention was to create a positive experience for every coworker interaction. Sharing a friendly hello or asking if there's anything you can do to help may not seem like much—but it adds up to something much greater. As you think about making an impact, remember the small, daily actions that make the office a happier place for your colleagues.

It seems like every day more research emerges to support positive psychology's relevance in all facets of life. The premise is simple: make happiness part of whatever you're doing. Studies show that we don't become happy upon achieving something, because we just shift the goal to something else. Instead, there are things you can do to train yourself to participate fully in each moment and therefore feel enriched from day to day. And while money is nice, it isn't what leads to fulfillment. In business, positive psychology has shown that we like meaningful work that, yes, takes effort, but that very fact is what makes it valuable to us.[14] Keep this in mind as you work to boost your career: you might achieve your goal, but you'll be even happier when you infuse the process of getting there with positivity.

Working with people who are optimistic and upbeat makes for better work results, fosters more creativity, and relieves work stress. Both recipients and the person spreading the good "karma" have better health and better work reviews. So read up on work by positive psychology experts like Martin Seligman and Mihaly Csikszentmihalyi. Not only will you learn to feel happier, but you will also authentically uplift everyone around you. Truly, the best kind of attention you can receive from other people are appreciation and gratitude.

PROPELLANT #4: TEAMWORK MAKES THE BUSINESS WORLD GO ROUND

While "two heads are better than one" is an old-school adage, it's more true today than ever before. Research attests that teams are most productive because they stimulate original thought and propose new approaches. It would be impossible to efficiently produce technology and manufacture all the gadgets and widgets and bonnets the world needs without effective teamwork. Businesses wouldn't survive. Teamwork often spans the globe and happens round the clock. With all these moving parts busy innovating and disrupting, established organizations co-existing with startups, and solitary workers renting offices in collaborative, community, "co-work spaces," it's easy to see that teamwork is just how things get done today. Mechele calls this seismic movement "coolaboration." And to do it well, there are things you need to keep high in mind.

People Feel Valued When You Listen to Them

If you're eager to impress a team, you may end up doing much more talking than listening. I should know because when I was young, my goal was to answer questions before they were asked. I thought that was what I needed to do to make an impact at my company and get ahead. Little did I know that my colleagues felt like I was talking over them and it was damaging my relationships. One day, my boss sat me down and told me he was sending me to a listening skills course to help me overcome my habit of dominating conversations. Well, I heard that message loud and clear. My newfound self-awareness allowed me to see my boss was pulling for me and thought I could change. He helped me to take a step back and better understand how listening makes people feel valued.

At every step of forming, maintaining, and making the most of collaborative relationships, it's vital to make people feel valued. They're also eager to make a reverberant impact, so their input and feedback can help you along the way. Listen to them. Reaching any goal that involves other people's skills, time, or buy-in starts with being a good listener. Communication is a two-way street, but listening is often more important than talking. By listening, you communicate your willingness to take in, consider, and apply what other people have to offer. So turn off your interruption button and demonstrate how collaborative you can be. Listening is a leadership skill and asset.

Respect Everyone's Workload

Work requires us all to juggle tasks and timelines, so be respectful of other people's commitments and priorities. Remember that your coworkers have other responsibilities outside of collaborating with you, and try as they may, their priorities might not align. That doesn't mean colleagues think your project is unimportant. It doesn't mean they aren't good team members. Especially if you are a manager, they may rely on you to rearrange their deadlines and their time usage to free them up to work on your project. Great leaders make an impact through keeping workloads sustainable and realistic. Pushing people to their limits and working them to the bone only decreases morale and ultimately increases turnover. So keep your expectations for people's contributions real. Encourage them and let them know your priorities by helping lighten their load somewhere else.

It's important to note that you won't always get a team behind your efforts. No matter how interesting and clever a new project or idea may be, some of your coworkers simply might not have the bandwidth to get involved. To determine whether you can gain the support of your team, you need to consider competing priorities, budget, and other commitments. If you can't corral support, that's okay. As you'll see in the next chapter, there are other meaningful ways you can make an impact on your own.

The Team Is More Important Than Winning or Losing

The reality is: things don't always work out. When your team doesn't reach its goals, gifted leaders don't point fingers and single someone out as the problem—and they don't tolerate that behavior from coworkers. They focus on maintaining the team's integrity and solidifying their loyalty for the next challenge that's certain to come.

Competitive athlete and Harvard graduate student Tom Randall is an expert on teamwork. As an undergrad football player and Olympic hopeful bobsled star, he knows that team members are under pressure to perform at their best. Even with incredible external pressure to succeed, high performers are their own harshest critics. So when they come up short of their goals, the last thing they need is to be singled out as a weak link on the team. Although most teammates understand this, Tom has seen how emotions can get the best of people after a tough loss, when the unfortunate reaction is to go after an individual who hasn't performed. In cases when this has happened, Tom says a good coach or team leader would step in. "I've seen people get crucified for pointing their finger after a tough loss," he said. "You don't go after one person. If you're on a good team, no one will single you out and blame you. You win as a team and you lose as a team."[15]

People respond to criticism in the office the same way athletes respond on the field. If you're already doing the best you can, being taken to task by a leader or peer is only going to make things worse. Most of the time, people already know what they did wrong and what they would they do differently next time. If a discussion is needed, it's best to have it after emotions have cooled down, and wherever possible privately, one on one, with the just you and the person who didn't rally. In those cases, one way to get the best outcome is to start the conversation with "What do you think we need to get out of our meeting today?" Making the issue about the two of you, on the same side against the problem, is reassuring, noncombative, and proactive.

One secret to a long-term, successful career is that your defining moments won't just be your successes. You will also be remembered by how you reacted when things went wrong. If you let your emotions get the best of you, it will damage relationships and make it harder to work with those people in the future. You may also gain a reputation for being difficult to work with, which is a real tough one to overcome. It can hinder your efforts for years. Bottom line: it pays to be a team player and, if you mess up, quickly admit your error. If someone else messes up, ask them if they're doing okay and help them get their confidence back ASAP.

PROPELLANT #5: LEARN FROM THE BEST, AND SHARE YOUR BEST, THROUGH MENTORING

We never stop learning. And sometimes we don't realize what we know until we have to teach it. Both learning and teaching are powerful ways to make a one-on-one, meaningful impact in your company. Knowledge transfer is key to any organization's stability. Newbies need to be onboarded quickly and efficiently, and turnover or layoffs shouldn't cause productivity to lag because the remaining employees don't know how to fill in the gaps. The generations need to support each other. Cultural values are more vibrant when they are directly told to incoming employees. And for employees to grow ever upward, they need the inside story on how to succeed within the company.

When Mechele started her first job after business school, she reported to two different VPs who both became mentors to her. They were very different people who taught her entirely different things. One was highly organized and went out of his way to give her tactical tips to help her succeed. He would share advice on how to better connect with sales reps and customers, build authentic relationships, and follow through to establish a reputation for caring about her customers' businesses. Mechele followed his advice. His tactical knowhow led to her acceptance as a team player. She gained respect by performing ahead of most of the cotrainees in her division.

The other VP's approach helped her too. He taught Mechele how to be a good leader just from the way he listened and spoke to his team. He built her confidence by letting her know that her ideas mattered. He would come into work in the morning and say, "Isn't this the best? *We* are running this organization!" His attitude was so contagious, his enthusiasm and belief in his people so unbridled, that he inspired Mechele to do her best work. She still thinks of him every time she talks to a new team or to a new hire, and she tries to bring them the positive energy and good vibes that her mentor imbued in her years ago.

These two VPs were both good at different things, rather than being good at everything. They shared their strengths with younger employees like Mechele and became incredibly memorable and motivating mentors. You too can benefit from a diversity of mentors, and you too can pass along your strengths.

Have you seen the public service announcements on TV that encourage dads to get more involved in parenting? They share the message that you don't have to be perfect to be a good parent—instead it's about doing what you can and making the effort. The same is true for being a mentor. Don't get stuck wondering if you have enough knowledge to help younger or less-tenured coworkers. Don't think you have nothing to contribute. The truth is that just about everyone has something valuable to teach others. You don't need all the answers to mentor well. You can be at any level, in any team, at any company. After all, you got where you are somehow. People would benefit from hearing your story, and you would benefit from hearing theirs. Taking the time to just listen awhile and share what you know, however simple that may seem, creates a positive impact on others. Depending on how and what you teach, as Mechele's story shows, your impact can last a lifetime.

When you become a mentor, even to casually share your knowledge with a coworker, you can focus on what you're good at and leave out the rest. Be humble and make it known that you don't have all the answers—but when it comes to XYZ, you know your stuff. And make questions part of your mentorship. "Do you get what I mean?" "Is there a way you would handle this differently?" "Is there something making you uncomfortable or feeling not connected?" "Is there a question bugging you?" It's this kind of gentle probing, without judgment, that makes a mentor a trusted influence.

Don't let misconceptions about age or tenure get in the way of a great relationship. Even younger, less-experienced employees can make excellent mentors for older employees to show them, for example, the ins and outs of the new digital landscape in the workplace. In fact, some companies, like Target, UnitedHealth Group, and Cisco Systems have found success with formal reverse mentorship programs.[16] Many millennials have been teaching older family members the nuts and bolts of technology for years, so helping older coworkers comes more naturally than some companies realize. My ad agency instituted "reverse mentorship" back in the nineties, in which coworkers met regularly after work to share knowledge. The program became one of the most compelling attractions to new hires, because they could perceive the many social and educational benefits

On the flip side, when you're looking for mentors, remember that you can zero in on learning-specific skills from different people. When you notice people doing something particularly well, pay them a sincere compliment and say with a smile that you're working on becoming better at that skill. Chances are they'll proactively give you some advice. To learn even more, offer to treat people to coffee or lunch if they will take the time to share some insight. These casual interactions build helpful relationships that can blossom into long-term mentorships.

PROPELLANT #6: THE MAGIC OF DIVERSITY HAPPENS THROUGH INCLUSION

It isn't enough for organizations to employ a diverse workforce. Minority employees, including women, must be given the same opportunities to advance as their colleagues. Most organizations say they support an equal opportunity environment, but in reality, this effort often falls flat. Why? A major factor is the underdeveloped relationships between minorities and nonminorities. The best leaders understand that minority workers need extra support to be included in the organizational culture and to connect with the people who can help them succeed. If you want to make an impact in today's business environment, be inclusive.

Kelsey is a scientist and a tenure-track professor at a well-respected university. She's also an outsider in what feels like a boys' club. When Kelsey was in college, there were equal percentages of men and women, but after grad school, women became underrepresented. The vast majority of her colleagues are men, which greatly affects the workplace culture and the opportunities for building relationships. In her male-dominated field, social activities that build comradery and provide networking opportunities skew toward things that appeal to men. In these situations, it can be especially difficult for women to form the same quality bonds with male coworkers. "I don't think they intentionally shut women out, but it can feel like that," Kelsey said, recalling an industry conference when her male colleagues went out to drink craft beer without considering whether she would want to join. "Men form 'bromances' in science. It's hard not to feel marginalized sometimes."

Being an outsider is about more than just feeling left out—you can actually miss out on career opportunities. Kelsey works in an industry where the goal of gaining tenure depends on doing collaborative, interdisciplinary research. Scientists collaborate with one another to produce something better than they could do alone. But to do that research, they need to proactively assemble a team. So by not being invited to drink beer with the guys, Kelsey misses out on the opportunity to form the bonds that become the basis for successful new research.[17]

Similar problems arise anytime you are left out of unofficial social activities with colleagues. Playing golf with the management team is about a lot more than eighteen holes. It's a chance for face time with people who can help advance your career. Whether it's during golf or lunches or happy hours, they offer pleasant banter, a solution to a problem you've been having, or advice on navigating the unwritten political rules for getting ahead at the company. So missing out on those casual conversations can be a serious career-path inhibitor. Unfortunately, it can be hard for people to understand how detrimental it is to be left out at work if they've never actually been left out.

Marvin learned this the hard way. After graduating from business school, he got a job at one of the "Big Four" accounting firms in the risk management group. This area of finance happens to be especially popular in China. In fact, out of the forty-some employees working in the Manhattan office, only a handful weren't Chinese. Being an American white male, Marvin couldn't remember a situation when he was the minority. He thought his new working environment would be an interesting "global business" experience, and he was optimistic about it. But he had trouble forming the same level of comradery that he'd enjoyed in past jobs, and it affected his mood and temperament throughout the day. It didn't help that his colleagues and his boss often spoke to one another in Chinese. Marvin even learned that his boss had parties at his house to celebrate

Chinese holidays and invited all his direct reports—except the three employees who weren't Chinese. One day, out of the blue, Marvin's previous employer called him up and made him an offer to come back. There were numerous reasons he took the offer, but an emotional factor was that he was sick of feeling like an outsider at work.

The experience wasn't all bad, because it opened his eyes to what it feels like to be excluded at work: extraordinarily demotivating. "It was something I was previously unaware of, but I now definitely take notice when it's happening to other people," Marvin said. He makes an effort to avoid being part of a clique that might seem off limits to some of his coworkers. His disconnected experience as an outsider brought a new level of sensitivity to the way he handles relationships at work, and he does everything he can to stay inclusive.[18]

Disbanding the boys' club or other workplace cliques isn't just the right thing to do, it's the way to drive the best outcomes. Widening your circle at work opens doors for you to better understand your coworkers' strengths and work with them more effectively. The more productive relationships you form, the more you learn, the smarter you become, and the more supportive fuel you receive. Try the following tips to be more inclusive at work.

Advice to Outsiders: Start conversations with colleagues you don't usually talk to. Make it known subtly that you would like to be included in social activities. Show interest in what your coworkers are doing, even if it isn't something you would choose to do on your own. Use your creativity, and ask your "insider" coworkers to do something as a group that you know they'd enjoy. This can help you become integrated in the social circle.

Advice to Insiders: Reflect on whether your relationships with certain colleagues are unintentionally excluding other colleagues. People form natural bonds based on shared interests, but the most successful leaders are inclusive rather than cliquey. Include marginalized coworkers when you're making lunch plans or considering who to partner with on a project. With them on board, your collective skillset will broaden and so will your strengths.

Advice to Managers: Take stock of your own actions as well as those of your team members. It is your responsibility to cultivate an amicable working environment where everyone has an equal opportunity to thrive. So foster friendly, casual relationships and mentoring that include all. If you see cliques forming, put the kibosh on it by pairing people up from different social circles for projects. At team meetings, congratulate cross-fertilization and model this positive behavior yourself. If a direct report is being left out, talk to your other reports about the importance of an inclusive team environment. And don't hesitate to meet with your HR director and superiors to ask about other ways you can help. Your efforts will not go unnoticed.

When it comes to making an impact at work, inclusion comes down to one thing: being a statesperson who is known for bringing people together. By striving to be part of an inclusive team rather than just a diverse one, you are sure to produce better outcomes and be noticed for it.

PROPELLANT #7: NETWORKING TIPS THAT BOOST YOUR EFFORTS

If you had a dollar for every time you heard someone talk about the importance of networking, you'd be rich. For that reason, we won't dive too deep on why networking is important for boosting your career. Instead, we'll focus on tips to get better at it.

Even Introverts Can Connect Authentically

For introverts, networking can be especially frustrating. Not everyone is hardwired to schmooze effortlessly with strangers over a drink at the end of an industry conference or even among colleagues after work. If reserved is your style, you're certainly not alone: more than a third of the population is introverted. Luckily, networking is something you can get better at with practice. The not-so-secret secret to networking is to identify what genuinely interests you about people—and pursue it.

Mechele is an example. She wasn't a great networker when she started out, mostly because she didn't have much experience in it and didn't understand the importance of it. But when friends got promotions or exciting new jobs, Mechele would ask how they did it. Most of the time, it had a lot to do with connections and delivering performance above expectations. They didn't get handed things because they knew the right people, but it did get their names in the hat. As Mechele talked with more people and heard more stories about how they got ahead, she realized her native interest in "career tales" became a fundamental part of how she formed connections. And in the process, she gained insight from listening to and learning about other people's job journeys. Essentially, she was networking before she even realized she was doing it.

When your intention to connect with people is pure, networking will come much more naturally than if you try to form calculated links with people who you hope can help you. Rather than plotting how to steer the conversation a certain way, cast your personal agenda aside so you can be fully present in your interactions. Get to know others just for the sake of enjoyable human interaction. Don't forget to keep a slight smile on your face, since a welcoming countenance counts. People will sense your authenticity.

Come Up with Connecting Points

Sometimes it helps to have a networking conversation starter. When Marcus was in business school at the University of Chicago, he was living off campus and wasn't meeting very many people outside his night classes. As an introvert, he struggled with networking. This was frustrating because he likely crossed paths with U of C students and alumni all the time. He knew it would be easy to strike up conversations if he could identify that connecting point. Marcus's girlfriend bought him U of C shirts as a conversation starter. She jokingly called them his "networking shirts," but it was no longer a joke when they actually worked. When Marcus wore the shirts around Chicago, all kinds of people would initiate conversations with him. "My wife just graduated from there. How do you like it?" "I teach at U of C. Are you a current student?" "Class of '04! How bout you?" It worked like a charm.[19]

Share Yourself So Others Share with You

You don't need to be a billboard for all your affiliations, but it's a great way to start relationships based on shared experiences and interests. Take the time to consider your personal life and ways you can bring it into your office space. Doing so will help people get to know you. Here are some ideas to kick off your brainstorm.

- If you're a proud alum working in a distant city, say an Ohio State grad who got a job in NYC, putting up a Buckeye decal in your cube or wearing an OSU cap is a sure way to get any fellow graduates or Ohioans to stop and chat.
- Concert or band posters are great connecting points, as whole subcultures arise from fans. You might hear some great stories from live events held around the country or throughout the world.
- Cartoons can express your style of humor. There is no better conversation starter than a laugh.
- If you have a favorite painter, frame some prints. One designer scanned vintage Italian posters and made a screensaver that people love to stop, watch, and comment on.

- Hobbies like knitting or woodworking lend themselves to displays. Bring in some of your work to showcase. When a software developer built an oak standing desk, it was so well made that everyone walking past his cube paused to admire it.
- Bring in samples of something you collect. If you restore and show vintage cars, bring photos. And in every office, there is the bobble-head collector, whose cubicle is so amusing that you must stop for a laugh on your way by.

You can't know where these relationships will end up going, and you don't need to. The important thing is that you're meeting new, and hopefully interesting, people and building your network.

Emphasize Quality over Quantity

Instead of focusing on the quantity of your connections, continuously build up the quality of relationships. Once you make new connections, maintain contact with them. This is pretty easy when you work at the same company, but it's more challenging if you can't simply run into them in the hallway. We get so busy with our jobs and personal lives that checking in with people to say hello isn't a top priority. Even professionals who are adept at building their networks can struggle to keep in touch. There's no urgent need to reach out to someone, and before you know it, years have passed. Although you're still connected on LinkedIn, is that person really in your network? Could you reach out and ask for advice on a project or recommendations for additional staff? Be prepared— you might not get a response.

So take the time to check in with past colleagues, former bosses, old classmates, favorite teachers, long-distance friends, and supportive relatives. Get into the habit of making two calls a week to people in your circle. Congratulate them when you see they've received a promotion or had a work anniversary. Stay in touch with an occasional business-related joke or cartoon. Use your social media platforms to comment on their status updates and posts or to retweet them. And ask people to meet for coffee or lunch every once in a while.

This doesn't just apply to your inner circle. Your cousin might casually mention that she knows someone who's investing in your dream startup. Or that Kai found a vendor who has a fix for a problem you long to resolve. You'd only find out that Jacob has just gotten approval to bring in someone with your skillset if you're on his radar. This outer circle of acquaintances could surprise you. Text, call, email, post, send a snapchat . . . whatever—just make the effort to keep up with their backgrounds and interests. You just might end up collaborating with them on your new project.

MOMENTUM-BUILDING STRATEGIES

Relationships are the most important thing within an organization. The reason for this is basic: any company can have plenty of smart and talented people, but to make an impact in the marketplace, it needs positive, productive relationships among its employees to get things done. And more broadly, among the professional community, relationships bring support, insight, and lessons in surprising ways that can fuel your launch. So as you aim high and explore how to get there, see every encounter as something meaningful to cultivate. Here are the strategies to keep in mind.

- Meaningful work helps the people around you.
- People will sense your genuine interest in them, so keep it real.
- Make yourself valuable to as many people as possible by helping them reach their goals.
- Become known for bringing people together and building all-inclusive, supportive teams.
- See building a network of quality relationships as essential fuel for your career.

3

Project Ideas to Spark Your Ignition

YOU HAVE THE PLATFORM FOR YOUR CAREER launch in place—you know how to identify the work that will turn heads at your organization. And you're all fueled up by cultivating the relationships that will get you where you want to go. Now it's time to choose the meaningful projects you can do to stand out, get recognized, and give your career that boost you need.

We asked all kinds of professionals for their secrets, and this chapter is filled with ways in which the people we interviewed stood out, added value, and became essential to their companies and its customers. In this chapter, you'll find eighteen meaningful projects that have been proven to make an impact by young professionals, seasoned managers, and people who are now senior executives looking back. CEOs, SVPs, VPs, executive directors, and entrepreneurial disrupters across a wide range of fields also shared what their employees have done that earned resounding accolades and advancement. We amassed these success stories, researched the practical tips you need to apply them, and now offer them to you as career-boosting projects.

We recommend checking out the projects one by one and flagging the ideas that fit your needs right now, as well as the ones that could be useful down the road. You'll read an overview of each project, then see the value behind it, discern what situations it is best executed within, measure the timeframe it takes to deploy, estimate the amount of work required, avoid common errors along the way, and determine exactly who will benefit in addition to you. This is all part of your course of action.

Each project is completely customizable to your organization's needs and your personal skillset and passions. They can all be done a variety of ways, applied repeatedly, and completed in ways that have both immediate and long-term impact. No matter your industry, skill level, or tenure, you will find a variety of projects that—as you work on them—will work for you.

Here's a list of the career-boosting projects that we gathered:

1. Lead "War Game" Exercises
2. Turn Your Direct Reports into Five-Star Performers
3. Connect Better—Upgrade Your Messaging
4. Maximize Your Personal Presence
5. Recognition Is the Secret Sauce
6. Be a Hero for Sorting Out a Mess
7. Launch a High-Interest Group and Have Fun Together
8. Gift Your Knowledge and Mentor
9. Do Unto Others . . . Pay It Forward
10. Reach Beyond Assumptions—Become a Value Engineer
11. Ace Networking to Build Your "Personal" Brand
12. Gather Customer Feedback—and Use It
13. Turn Prospects into Clients Faster
14. Stay Current—Update Your Website
15. Get Social Media Savvy and Get Known
16. Do Good, Give Back, and Thrive All-Round
17. Check the Cultural Climate and Set a Better Temperature
18. Transcend the Silo Mindset to Think Big

CAREER-BOOSTING PROJECT #1: LEAD "WAR GAME" EXERCISES

Anticipate your opponent's next move by putting yourself in their shoes. Think General Patton versus General Rommel. Patton ultimately defeated him by researching every battle Rommel fought and analyzing how his underlings wrote their battle plans. He was then poised to make his own winning moves. By taking your blinders off, doing competitive research, and objectively assessing how your product or service compares, you'll uncover hidden weaknesses—both theirs and yours—and potential threats. How could a competitor "attack" in a way that would do you the most damage? How can you outflank a rival's move by introducing a new product, feature, or service? Would reallocating some resources give you flexibility to counter an offensive? Consider the pros and cons of recruiting a key individual from your competitor or a former employee. You'll learn a lot as you consider these things and more.

Your Course of Action

Amount of work required: Medium

Timeframe for completion: This project can be done in a single meeting or it can turn into a larger project applicable to multiple products or services. Taking some time to prepare market research and analytics ahead of time will spark your colleagues to come up with new insights and tactics.

When to execute: Your competitors are nipping at your heels. You've had a comfortable place in the industry for a while, but you're worried about disruption. Your team is stuck in a rut and having trouble innovating. You want to find a creative way to jump-start sales. This project will help you find innovative solutions to all these problems.

Support needed: To get the best results, you need to invite to your war-game exercise a diverse group of individuals who represent different departments. Look to your top salespeople for data and opinions, and possibly hire a brainstorming consultant to rev up the idea hive.

The "real boss" this will impress: Senior leaders are particularly impressed when employees show strategic-thinking skills and a passion for expanding market share.

Benefits to organization: This project can produce game-changing ideas, ones that spark innovative approaches to business as usual. It also positively impacts corporate culture by engaging employees and soliciting their input.

Benefits to you: It demonstrates your creativity and your approach as a team player. It shows that you look to the future by analyzing current trends, anticipating the way change happens. You could even kick-start beneficial changes with this project, which could have a cascading effect.

Cost: Free, unless you choose to hire an outside consulting firm for ancillary brainpower.

Potential challenges: Your team may come up with great ideas or recommendations for new approaches, but strategy is valued subjectively. You may need approval from higher-ups. Before you get started, make sure everyone understands that the process is to come up with competitive ideas. These will be written up or presented to senior leaders for approval.

Options for future enhancements: When your team learns how to work with the competition in mind and applies the "War Game" mentality on an ongoing basis, you'll all generate revenue-producing ideas more aggressively.

CAREER-BOOSTING PROJECT #2: TURN YOUR DIRECT REPORTS INTO FIVE-STAR PERFORMERS

The upper echelons look at your staff and see direct reflections of you. So be a great leader, at any level, and develop your team. Assess your reports. Take a good look at each person's strengths, career development potential, engagement, grasp of long-term goals, and promotability. Brainstorm ways to motivate and support success. Have open discussions with individual team members about their interests and passions. From that vantage point, you can uncover new opportunities to increase motivation and productivity and help each person fulfill his or her goals. Then find ways to act on all this information. This project could also open your eyes to the reality that someone is unmotivated, underperforming, or causing more interpersonal challenges than advantages. It's better to look at their future with clear eyes and possibly think of how and when you need to let that C-player go. This project will build your reputation as a manager who is interested in—and actively supports—job satisfaction and growth. Being known for this attracts talented people who lift you as you lift them.

Your Course of Action

Amount of work required: This depends on how large your team is, how comfortable you are having career development conversations with them, and the ways you come up with to help them hone their skills. You can invest as much time and energy in this project as resources allow.

Timeframe for completion: Ideally, this is an ongoing project, rather than a one-off exercise. Set aside a timeslot each week to dedicate yourself to assessing and brainstorming ways to bring out the best in everyone.

When to execute: You're new at managing and want to set high standards for your team. A direct report is coming up short in performance or presence. You want to get promoted but need a qualified candidate to fill your current shoes. You were assigned a new team and need to get to know them. A big project is on the horizon and you want to position everyone to achieve the best results.

Support needed: Unless you've gotten feedback that your reports need more support from you, this is a project you can initiate on your own without approval from higher-ups. As a manager, developing your team's skillset is part of your job description. It does help to have training from a smart mentor or HR professional on how to have effective career-development talks with your direct reports. While new managers should be trained on this from the get-go, it's common to have to seek it out. So ask the right people or do your own research. When you decide on the logistics for this project (having weekly meetings with reports, daily status updates, or setting specific goals), your direct reports will be active participants in their own development. If you run into issues you can't solve together, you may need your boss's guidance.

The "real boss" this will impress: Because your reports fall under your direct supervisor's branch of the hierarchy, this will make him or her look good also. And this will reflect on your direct reports, since you'll be working with them more closely on career development. HR staffers will also notice, as they're invested in people doing well.

Benefits to organization: Increases employee engagement, productivity, and effectiveness; prevents costly and time-consuming turnover.

Benefits to you: Work can be so much more productive when you have a passionate team of people behind you. You'll be able to delegate work and know it will be done the right way and on time. You look good to other leaders in the company. Positive talent-management skills give you increased job security. You will be trusted to lead bigger teams and advance within the organization because you've clearly demonstrated your leadership ability to the right people.

Cost: Free to low cost. There could be continued education and enrichment costs for your reports, such as webinars, seminars, training workshops, or biweekly "lunch and learn" meetings. Leaders never stop teaching—and learning too.

Potential challenges: When you put time and effort into developing people, and they don't improve, you will be faced with the decision to part ways with them or give them additional coaching. It's also possible that your reports will gain career capital, making it easier for them to move on to another department or company. **Options for future enhancements:** This career-boosting project has a lot of room to expand. Your reports will always have room to grow, and there are countless methods for coaching, training, and mentoring them. On the flip side, if any of your reports aren't responding well to your guidance or one-on-one coaching, you'll need to part ways. Unmotivated, negative players will only hurt your team. It's better to hire a new rock star report than try to motivate people who aren't invested in their own growth.

CAREER-BOOSTING PROJECT #3: CONNECT BETTER—UPGRADE YOUR MESSAGING

All relationships are supported by quality communication. When you want to reach people, say it right, say it clearly, and say it simply. The best way to know if you are achieving this is to get feedback on your messaging and branding. Are you actually conveying things as well as you hope you are? See your imprint from colleagues' perspectives. Take a step back and think about how clients and customers interpret the messages you're sending.

Are your texts or emails engaging and clear? Do your monthly product updates cover what people want to know? Are your sales reports offering data in a way everyone understands? Do you use a little creativity to get your point across? No matter what department you work in, you can improve and upgrade any form of communication. Interactive vehicles you can use to repair and upgrade your messaging include: internal brainstorming meetings, focus groups with customers and noncustomers to discover what's important to them, analysis of your competitors' approaches, and informal conversations. Challenge yourself to better understand your stakeholders' needs and wants so you can upgrade the ways you reach out to them.

Your Course of Action

Amount of work required: This project is highly scalable. You can make an impact by rewriting a single piece of brand communication that is in desperate need of a refresh. This can be done entirely in house or in collaboration with an ad agency. You can also spearhead a revamp of all client-facing documents after conducting a different kind of market research. Think like the late Steve Jobs and Amazon's Jeff Bezos: focus on customers' *wants*—not just needs. Or you could simply reformat your weekly report, add more diagrams, or decrease in-speak and industry jargon to write more directly.

Timeframe for completion: Depends entirely on the project scope.

When to execute: Important communication pieces haven't been updated for a long time and no longer fit how your company or department has evolved. Products, services, or policies have changed but your messaging about them hasn't. Your department is having a hard time communicating effectively with clients or other departments. You have not yet reached out for feedback on new messaging. You notice general room for improvement—misplaced apostrophes, spelling errors, awkward sentences, incorrect terminology, loaded jargon—you name it.

Support needed: You may need to get approval to facelift certain communications. Seek feedback from colleagues on their communication irritants, and involve them for a project with larger scope. You may have in-house designers and copywriters to draw on, or you could hire freelancers. Mechele and I bring in a great editor to enhance our efforts. This helps us keep messaging fresh while staying focused on other aspects of our businesses.

The "real boss" this will impress: Your own boss will be impressed by your initiative and passion for keeping messaging clear and current. Your target audiences, including key customers, will benefit. And you could attract new clients.

Benefits to organization: Improving brand image, both internally and externally, refreshes the entire company. Ensures customers and prospects receive current and accurate information. Helps people and teams work together more effectively.

Benefits to you: Shows that you know even little things count when making an impression. Proves your communication and writing skills. Demonstrates vision, attention to detail, and commitment to quality.

Cost: Free, unless you want to expand this into a major project and hire an outside consulting firm to assist with market research, copywriting, or new content creation.

Potential challenges: Sometimes changes that seem simple can require a long and drawn-out approval process. This is a common quagmire when upgrading messaging in large companies, because it portrays the face of the company and is very important. So senior executives will want to weigh in—heavily. These multiple, high-level decision makers can make this collaborative effort very difficult to keep on track. Before you start this project, make sure you identify the influentials who need to be involved. You don't want to include more people than necessary, but you don't want to upset any key managers by leaving them out of the loop. The challenge is that communication strategy is subjective, so there will be a lot of opinions. And the final product may be a lot different from what you started with.

Some changes can be objective, such as typos, grammar, punctuation, and incorrect, outdated, or redundant information. It's easier to upgrade those. Also, if your company has a brand voice, you can make an argument that certain communications materials don't offer the official tone. For example, if the brand voice is light and casual, you could update a document for clients to match that tone. Other good ways to combat subjectivity is by making a case with market research or the authority of an ad agency, brand consultant, or your marketing and sales VPs. Just be sure everyone supports the changes.

Options for future enhancements: Content needs to stay fresh, whether it's internal or external. But even small organizations have trouble keeping their messaging up to date across all its numerous mediums. If you can help your organization communicate more effectively, you're making a huge impact. A lot of people have poor writing skills and don't enjoy it, so if you have the knack, you can carve a great niche for yourself—no matter what department or field you are in. People will be impressed.

CAREER-BOOSTING PROJECT #4: MAXIMIZE YOUR PERSONAL PRESENCE

You can be talented, capable, reliable, and eager, but if all that isn't apparent when people first meet you, your presence isn't an asset to you or your organization. The way you show up is important. Your passion, demeanor, body language, style of speaking, interests, and appearance say a great deal about who you are as an individual and as a professional. Personal presence can make a huge difference in getting ahead. Focus on increasing your self-awareness about how others perceive you and maximizing your personal presence accordingly. There are a variety of ways to do this, and you can pick the options that work best for you.

- Join a group to hone your public speaking skills, such as Toastmasters.
- Retain a presentation skills coach.
- Record yourself giving a mock presentation and critique your own performance.
- Practice your thirty-second elevator pitch in the mirror to polish your explanation of your skills.
- Ask for feedback on your personal presence and speaking skills from a colleague or friend who's business savvy.

- Consult with a mentor.
- Read up on body language and presentation cues.
- Assess whether your wardrobe properly represents you as a professional and make any necessary changes.
- Clean up your desk, cube, car, or the area pictured on a video conference when you work from home.
- Hire a personal branding consultant or stylist to personally upgrade your look.
- Read up on business and dining etiquette.
- Put together and deliver a presentation (and video yourself first), and then present to your team or customers to get more on-the-job presentation experience.

You can consider these efforts "personal best" appointments with yourself. Put them in your calendar along with your goals and stick to them. No matter which options you choose to improve your presence, the aim is to view yourself and your work style through a different lens. Then make the adjustments needed to grow and be recognized. Be mindful to focus on your superior's expectations of you, and keep asking "How am I doing?"

Your Course of Action

Amount of work required: This project is scalable and depends on your current situation and how big the gap is between where you are and where you want to be.

Timeframe for completion: Devoting a couple of hours per week can result in noticeable improvements within a month's time.

When to execute: You struggle with shyness or fear of public speaking. You're fairly new to the business world and need to polish your professionalism. You worry that your coworkers don't take you seriously or underestimate your capabilities. You're surrounded by colleagues who have much more experience under their belts. Your desk or office is messier than your colleagues'. You are regularly asked to speak up, clarify, or repeat yourself. You've gotten feedback that you need to express more confidence. You've been overlooked for promotions and you're not sure why.

Support needed: This project is different from many of the others because it has a personal nature. If you want to improve your speaking skills, you can discuss that with your boss, but professional wardrobe and tidiness are another issue. Unless you've received feedback on these things already, work on them on your own time without bringing in your boss. You will need candid feedback from others to improve. Enlist people you trust, such as friends, family members, mentors, or an objective third party such as a personal branding coach.

The "real boss" this will impress: Everyone you interact with will notice your progress, especially those who have already mastered their personal presence and are therefore appreciative when others make the effort. These people can include colleagues, managers, VPs, C-suite executives, HR, and clients. This effort impacts everyone.

Benefits to organization: A robust presence garners trust, and trust is a cornerstone for effective teams. If you're in a customer-facing role, you will positively impact your organization's reputation and help increase sales and retention.

Benefits to you: Feel more confidence. Win greater respect from colleagues and superiors. Be considered a serious contender for advancement. Learn practical skills you can use for the rest of your career. Stay innovative. Make immediate and positive impressions that launch beneficial relationships.

Cost: Free to low. Many of these costs will need to come out of your pocket, but see this as an investment in yourself.

Potential challenges: When you are facing a change to how you have done things for a long time, it can feel quite chilling, like you are compromising your authenticity. You kind of like yourself as you are, and you don't want to turn into another person, but you always need to develop your professionalism, move forward, and become the best version of yourself. Be daring and visualize how you would sound, look, and be perceived once you've reached your ultimate career goal. That version of you may be even more authentic than the habits that hold you back.

It does take time to evolve your image. It's impossible to change people's impression of you overnight. And it might be hard to tell if people are perceiving you differently, but you can ultimately measure success by higher scores on performance reviews and 360-degree evaluations and through good feedback from your boss, higher-ups, colleagues, HR, customers, and friends. If you are feeling more confident overall, that's a great sign of progress.

Options for future enhancements: Professionals need to continue honing their personal presence throughout their careers, but when work gets busy, sometimes efforts can fall by the wayside. It's good to keep this project top of mind and stay alert to how others perceive you. Improved self-confidence will allow so many things to fall into place. You will have more opportunities to work directly with higher-level colleagues and clients, manage bigger projects, and be a presenter or organize the presentations at meetings. All of this will reap greater recognition.

CAREER-BOOSTING PROJECT #5: RECOGNITION IS THE SECRET SAUCE

People don't quit jobs as much as they quit managers. Keep your talent by showing direct reports how much you appreciate their contribution to the cause. Recognition is the number-one motivator of employee engagement, no matter the age or rank of the worker.[20] Mechele once had a very demanding boss who for years never uttered the words "thanks" or "good job." Then out of the blue, this boss started to express genuine gratitude. What a difference it made! Down went employee turnover and up went willingness to spend extra time tackling thorny challenges. It rippled throughout the team and was the best kind of example to set: that it's never too late to learn a new dance step.

If you manage millennials, recognition is especially important. Research shows that millennials want to be recognized multiple times each day. That might seem like a lot, especially to boomers or generation Xers, but millennials aren't looking for long sit-down meetings filled with gratitude. Most of the time they just want a simple "good job" to let them know you value their work and to serve as feedback that they are meeting your expectations. There are a variety of ways to celebrate a job well done.

- Ask your staff members privately if they appreciate public recognition. Some people are shy and don't like to be called out in a group setting, whereas other people live for that kind of glory. For the publicity adverse, ask them how they would like you to give them feedback.
- Take note when people do things well. Celebrate their success! Put congratulatory emails in a separate folder or jot down wins in a notebook. I send a general congratulatory email or text to each member on a team at the conclusion of a project and add a personal note of gratitude at the end. When you make it a point to be more aware of when people have done a good job, it will be easier to thank them later. The rapport with your team will grow.
- Make sure you use all your company's options for recognizing employees, such as: nominating them for company awards or bonuses, thanking them in monthly meetings, buying everyone coffee or helium balloons, planning a catered lunch for the team, and creating fun awards that acknowledge the qualities team leaders expressed along the way.
- Timing counts. When someone hits a homerun, show your appreciation in real time. If you follow up later with a hand-

written thank-you note, that makes your appreciation even more meaningful. The janitor at Mechele's company kept a five-year-old thank-you note from her on his bulletin board. Unfortunately, she found out about it after he passed away. If she had known how much he valued handwritten notes, she would have sent many more.

- People are motivated by having a sense of purpose. Tie recognition back to your organization's mission so that people are reminded of how they are contributing to big-picture success.

Your Course of Action

Amount of work required: Low.

Timeframe for completion: It might take a month or so for you to get into the regular habit of showing gratitude. This is what Mechele calls "exercising the thank-you muscle." Don't let up.

When to execute: Your team is suffering from burnout or turnover. You've received feedback that you are "rough around the edges" or otherwise difficult to work with. You do a gut check and realize you don't vocalize your gratitude regularly. You get the feeling that your direct reports are intimidated by you. You know that expressing emotions is challenging for you.

Support needed: It's helpful if your company has formal recognition processes, but if not, that shouldn't stop you from showing gratitude. And you don't need permission from a superior to implement this project. Unless you've received feedback that this is an area of improvement for you, it's probably best to work on this under the radar.

The "real boss" this will impress: Anyone you interact with will enjoy a more satisfying experience of working with you. Direct reports will benefit the most and, as they pay it forward, you will get the credit for cultivating such comradery.

Benefits to organization: Stern or intimidating bosses contribute to turnover, which is a major expense and a slowdown of progress. So by acknowledging your team's hard work, they'll be increasingly motivated, happy, engaged, and productive—all things that boost a company's success.

Benefits to you: When people find you agreeable to work with, more doors will open. You create a better case for being chosen for projects that could build your career. Colleagues will be able to communicate with you more openly, which naturally improves your team's effectiveness.

Cost: Free.

Potential challenges: If giving recognition hasn't been easy for you, a sudden switch could seem forced. It could feel like a struggle to establish this habit so that it feels and appears authentic. If this is the case, it's best to develop the gratitude muscle by reflecting on the positive things people have done. As the brilliant business coach Dale Carnegie wrote in the 1940s, be "hearty in your approbation and lavish in your praise."[21] It's career changing.

If you are someone who has high standards and want people to meet them, you need to let them know they're on track. Watch out for your own perfectionism, as expecting people to fulfill everything you desire is unrealistic. Stick to giving out sincere thanks, and leave off what they could have done better. Let them bask under your umbrella of appreciation for a full minute.

When you change your behavior, it can take time for people to realize that improvements weren't just rare flukes. Be patient and persist. This is a great way to bring out the best in people by reinforcing it when you see their best being demonstrated.

Options for future enhancements: There is a plethora of creative ways to recognize others and make them feel valuable. If your company doesn't have formal programs, you can spearhead your own program. Speak with some of your bright colleagues for ideas.

CAREER-BOOSTING PROJECT #6: BE A HERO FOR SORTING OUT A MESS

Over time, a little disorganization can turn into mammoth-sized chaos. Without good procedures for keeping things organized—and especially if people ignore procedure—things can get out of hand quickly. Chances are, everyone knows when something is a mess, but no one wants to take it on. This project has high visibility and can make things better for a lot of people. When you take on a tedious task other people want done but don't want to volunteer to do themselves, you emerge as a hero. Supervisors love volunteers. Efforts like this take away an irritant, discussed in chapter 1, which is among the best ways to make a meaningful impact. Here are some examples of messes in need of solutions.

- Reorganize a physical mess in the office. Think entrance, supply room, break room, storage locker, or filing cabinets.
- Organize and rename hard-to-find files. Talk to coworkers and create new files to house random documents. Post a "new file name" list to make things easier to find.
- Clean up your customer relationship management (CRM) system, or whatever strategy or technology you use to track interactions through the customer lifecycle. A good CRM system is incredibly valuable for understanding your customer base and how people are interacting with your company. The amount of data can make it a beast to manage. But the longer you wait to organize data, the worse it gets. If you can take the time to update contacts and get the right information in the right fields, it can be a huge accomplishment.
- If your company or department shares software to manage contacts, and you're getting returned mail, bouncing emails, or calls that are not going through, or you're stymied when wanting to reach out to someone, take on the task of updat-

ing it. Doing so offers a great opportunity to warm up those contacts.

- If your processes are in disarray, emails with status updates are overloading inboxes, or people need to be notified when it's their turn to work on something, look into project-management software. This will coordinate efforts so that anyone on a project can know its status through alerts or just a few clicks.

Your Course of Action

Amount of work required: Depends on what you're untangling.
Timeframe for completion: A couple of hours to weeks of work.
When to execute: You're annoyed with a source of disorganization that's impacting everyone's productivity. You're new at the job or unproven due to less experience and want to get noticed. You're a tenured employee who needs to show more initiative and get that much-needed pat on the back. You love organizing and derive a high level of satisfaction from systematizing and tidying up.
Support needed: Make sure you understand the problem and its ramifications before you start making changes that affect other people. Run your ideas for reorganizing by your boss and colleagues and ask for their input without laying blame on anyone in particular. This will prevent you from creating a neat and tidy system that no one else understands or wants. Take yourself lightly on this one, but take the task seriously. You may need to work on this project on your own time so that it doesn't get in the way of your daily responsibilities. Doing so will help gain your boss's support if she doesn't want to invest the team's time to fix a mess they didn't create.
The "real boss" this will impress: The impact can be big or small, but this project usually touches a lot of people.
Benefits to organization: Things run more smoothly and coworkers will no longer be exasperated. By removing the time navi-

gating a mess and providing a true fix for the problem, you can make a lot of people happy for the long run.

Benefits to individual: Get extra points for discreetly correcting something widely seen as tedious or unpleasant. Win recognition from superiors for stepping up and raising your hand first. People tend to be vocal about changes that make their job easier, so this project will put you in the limelight.

Cost: Free.

Potential challenges: If something has been a mess for a long time, there's probably a reason for it. Maybe one of the managers likes it as is, or he fears change . . . mostly the latter. Go to him with a plan that makes him look good and win "yes—move on it please!"

Options for future enhancements: Once you've completed this project, develop a system for staying organized. Motivate others to expand or contribute to what you've done. Monitor the state of whatever you untangled to make sure it doesn't get messy again.

CAREER-BOOSTING PROJECT #7: LAUNCH A HIGH-INTEREST GROUP AND HAVE FUN TOGETHER

Gather people around something you love to do. People who lead employee groups get known for being proactive achievers and for being capable leaders. They strive to make things better for cow-orkers by boosting comradery and creating friendships. There are so many possibilities in this project: yoga over lunch hour, lunch 'n' learn talks from experts, a book club, pick-up basketball or volleyball games, a group that conducts mock job interviews for returning vets, a crowd that goes walking on lunch breaks outside or at the mall, a Pokémon Go club, an a cappella singing group, a group that dabbles in all kinds of crafts, a team for an upcoming road race, a garden produce exchange, a kombucha-making club that gifts scobies to new members, a monthly potluck luncheon, or a skunkworks project team. If you have an interest, chances are other people do too. Go find them and have fun!

Your Course of Action

Amount of work required: Probably medium, but it depends on the group and whether the organizational responsibilities can be shared. There will be the times when you get together, and if you are leading the group, you will also need to prepare for it.

Timeframe for completion: Likely several months to a year or more.

When to execute: You want to meet more key people in your organization and build robust relationships. You have a specific interest and would like more responsibility around that interest. You want to share your personal interests with others diplomatically.

Support needed: To lead a group, you need other passionate colleagues who want to be involved. If a group is already going strong, it should be easy for you to become involved. If there aren't any groups that interest you, talk with coworkers to get a sense of what they would be interested in. Then create an idea that has organization-wide impact, e.g., skunkworks. Use that knowledge when you present your idea to your boss or HR supervisor.

The "real boss" this will impress: Your HR department takes special note of this kind of effort. Coworkers who have shared your interests will appreciate your leadership mentality.

Benefits to organization: Boosts coworker comradery and cultivates a positive, enriching culture. Makes the office about more than work.

Benefits to individual: You can become known for your smiling, proactive approach. Colleagues can become friends. You'll explore new personal interests and hopefully have fun!

Cost: Your group might not need funding to launch. If you want to plan something that does cost money, coworkers could pay their own way if the cost is minimal. Otherwise, there might be unallocated money in the budget for employee enrichment activities. Ask your supervisor.

Potential challenges: You might have a hard time keeping your coworkers interested and active in your new group, especially when things get busy at work. It's smart to use RSVPs to gauge their commitment to attending meetings and events, just in case you need to make any adjustments. Also be aware that planning group activities shouldn't be done on company time.

Options for future enhancements: Make sure your colleagues know about your group and all the great things it's doing and that they truly feel welcome to join. Keep it upbeat and focus on how fantastic the group is, rather than tooting your own horn about being a great group leader. Groups always have room to expand. One road race could turn into multiple races. A single potluck luncheon could turn into social time that coworkers want to have every week or a kick-starter for Meals on Wheels volunteering.

CAREER-BOOSTING PROJECT #8: GIFT YOUR KNOWLEDGE AND MENTOR

It is a proven fact: employees are more successful in the workplace when they have mentors to guide and support them. So pitch in to the big picture of success by offering your knowledge. And in the process, stay open to learning from your mentee's fresh ideas, generational wisdom, and technology usage. The very best mentoring relationships have two-way benefits. Here are some things you might have to offer.

- Model an attitude.
- Tell success stories and failure stories, with the lessons learned.
- Be candid about how you've navigated things like work-life balance.
- Share a specialized skill.

- Advise on projects or challenges.
- Help get someone up to date on the latest technology.
- Give honest feedback from hard-won experience.
- Share insights gleaned fresh from business school or colleagues.
- Contribute experience from another industry.
- Cross-pollinate ideas and processes by drawing on a variety of career experience.

Everyone benefits from mentoring—both in the giving and the receiving—which we discussed in depth in chapter 2. Most mentoring relationships form organically, and all it takes to formalize them is a conversation. Some organizations have programs established that pair people up; if yours does, speak with someone in HR to see who will benefit most from what you can offer.

Your Course of Action

Amount of work required: Low.

Timeframe for completion: Mentorships can be long-term, if not lifetime, relationships—bringing benefits that transcend companies, roles, specific projects and goals, distance, and even contact. The actual time spent in these exchanges can be regular or spontaneous and can consist of regular check-ins or occur on an as-needed basis. These don't require much time, and being too busy is not a valid excuse for falling out of touch. Contact can be as simple as chatting near the coffee machine or checking in with a call or email. Let your mentees know they can reach out to you at any time with questions. Show that you are happy to help them. As mentees grow, the amount of time you dedicate to them will most likely decrease. Any relationships that offer two-way benefits will endure the most.

When to execute: You don't currently have a mentee. You're great at something that causes other people to struggle. Colleagues frequently ask for your advice. You notice that new or younger employees are not getting the support or training they need to succeed in the organization.

Support needed: Organizations love mentoring and either actively encourage it or passively understand that it will happen naturally. So you don't need anyone's approval, but letting your boss know about the relationships shows your investment in big-picture success.

The "real boss" this will impress: You will impress senior leaders, HR, and your peers. You'll gain admiration from your mentees and make a huge impact in their lives. Their stardom will shine brightly on you.

Benefits to organization: Keeps knowledge transfer alive. Improves cross-generational relationships. Helps less-tenured employees carve a clearer career path within the organization, which increases retention. Drives performance of high-potential newbies.

Benefits to you: Don't just feel good about helping others, feel great about it. Make a long-term impact when people you coached turn into rock stars. Being a mentor can even become part of your personal brand: I was elated when I was named the 2015 Pharma Mentor of the Year by *PM360* magazine.

Cost: Free.

Potential challenges: When people look up to you, you have a greater responsibility to do the right things. You need to maintain credibility and integrity on a constant basis. If you say one thing but do another, you set a bad example for anyone working to emulate you. Additionally, relationships need to be nurtured to stay healthy and thrive. Mentorships shouldn't be a drain on time, but they do require a meaningful connection—which can be challenging when life gets busy.

Options for future enhancements: Your mentee's success is your success. When you become known as a knowledgeable pro who enjoys helping others, people start introducing you to friends, coworkers, and family members who need advice. It's genuinely flattering and can bear fruit in many ways, as your network will get boosts in both size and goodwill.

CAREER-BOOSTING PROJECT #9: DO UNTO OTHERS . . . PAY IT FORWARD

We can't emphasize this enough: a surefire way to boost your career is to help a wide variety of people. In today's working world, no job is isolated. Don't form a myopic vision of your role, even if you work from home or across the globe. Isolation will harm you in the long run. Instead, reach out. This collegiality leads to cooperation, innovation, productivity, and overall happiness. Everyone can more easily perceive solutions to problems that could be systemic to your organization. So get known by reaching out to help coworkers and become seen as a whole-company player.

This project begins by listing all the people in your company who you touch in your day-to-day work. You could collaborate a lot or occasionally; you may represent different phases in a product life cycle; their work may support yours or vice versa; or perhaps they pop up on your conference calls to share a point of view. Maybe your only contact point is that you pass their cubes on the way into the office every day or borrow from their product sample collection. List them all. Then take one, or all, of these approaches.

- List any pain points you know they have. Brainstorm ways you could help, even small efforts like volunteering to put that product sample collection back in order after everyone's pilfering. Or restock the receptionist's candy bowl, tell IT about a deal on a wish-list technology for the conference room, send marketing a link to a social platform you came across, forward articles you read that address challenges, or offer to review a report to contribute feedback from your department's point of view. The goal is simple: to uncover ways you can help. You will easily win recognition for this.

- If you aren't sure what you could do to help people far and wide, just ask. You could bring it up casually in the break room, via email, or by checking with your boss to see if she's aware of anything.
- Check in with a department you collaborate with and ask, "Hope I'm meeting your expectations? Is there anything else I can be doing?" This simple gesture of goodwill can go a very long way because, when you receive and integrate their feedback, both departments will benefit.

Your Course of Action

Amount of work required: High.

Timeframe for completion: You will help with a variety of one-off tasks, but overall, this is an ongoing project.

When to execute: You want to gain visibility with leaders in other departments (this is especially important if your company decides its promotions by group consensus or your department isn't located all in one place). You're concerned about being laid off from a merger or acquisition and need strong justification to show your team-player abilities. You need HR to register that you are on the team.

Support needed: You might need permission from your supervisor to spend extra time helping other departments' unresolved challenges. Use your best "higher-up" judgment on this one.

The "real boss" this will impress: Your peers, customers, and HR as well as leaders in other departments.

Benefits to organization: Everything runs more smoothly when people work well together across departments and job functions.

Benefits to individual: Become known as an employee crucial to the organization's efficiency and productivity. Form new relationships with influencers. Going above and beyond for colleagues naturally lends itself to getting noticed. Build your reputation for being a knowledgeable and helpful coworker. This course can prime you for a promotion or at least a lateral move to another desired department.

Cost: Time, and often lots of it, but it is commensurate with good outcomes and reviews.

Potential challenges: Managing your own workload when another department seeks your help with issues that your boss doesn't deem a priority. Missing timelines by agreeing to take on more than you can handle. Underperforming or underdelivering and doing your reputation more harm than good. Another challenge is being taken advantage of for your goodwill. Keep a log of the things you do to help other departments and stakeholders so that you know when your work contributed to a positive consequence. Also be conscious of and make a note when you help your peers and they don't make it known to their supervisor. You don't need to get credit for every single good deed, but it's important for leaders to know when you're actively contributing. To do this tactfully, you can casually ask a leader about a project you worked on, saying that you hope your input was helpful and productive and you're happy to help out again as needed.

Options for future enhancements: It's good to wear many hats, but don't put on so many that you lose your head! You can expand on this project, but not so much that it starts competing with your regular job duties. Stay focused. Multitasking has had its fifteen minutes of fame.

CAREER-BOOSTING PROJECT #10: REACH BEYOND ASSUMPTIONS—BECOME A VALUE ENGINEER

Don't get stuck in a rut, even when it comes to your bestselling products. This project gets you looking at everything from a fresh perspective—and we mean everything. Carefully examine a product, service, system, or process. Analyze its appeal, its presumed use, the working parts, and the needs it fulfills, and then think beyond those assumptions to come up with new approaches. Whether you end up eliminating something extraneous, adding a new promotional angle, or even expanding into a new market, you will be driving to improve what you're offering customers or stakeholders and bring cost savings to the company.

Mechele does this with her clients to help them come up with innovative strategies. For example, a cereal maker wants to create a new winner in their market space. Their product line is starting to feel dated, and they want to try something new. Mechele works with situations like this to deconstruct every aspect of the breakfast experience and ask, "Why do we do this?" The goal is to identify the aspects of the product that customers don't value and eliminate those aspects, and to highlight what they do value. To do this, the cereal team considers a series of questions along these lines:

- Does cereal have to be grain based?
- What's unnatural about it?
- What should be more natural?
- Who doesn't it appeal to?
- What would make consumers use it more?
- Does cereal have to be eaten in the morning?
- Do we have to eat it with a spoon?
- Is there a product we can eat on the go?

When you identify all existing assumptions, you start to see where they aren't necessary, where they overlook some customers' needs, and all the ways they hold back your market offerings. This can lead to a whole new product or the elimination of a costly process or ingredient. Here's another breakfast example: market researchers watched kids eating yogurt and saw that they tossed the spoon and napkin aside to eat faster. These researchers filmed kids squeezing the yogurt cup directly into their mouths. Someone at Yoplait had the bright idea to make it easier for them to do that. Tubular yogurt was born and given a meaningful name: "Go-Gurt."

Value engineering works on internal policies and procedures to help modify pesky irritants. It enables you to scrutinize every rule, every "our way or the highway" procedure, and it allows you to have an open debate about which ones are unnecessary, burdensome, or costly. For example, the company wants new talent. But you notice that corporate policy requires eight months of employment before new hires are entitled to half-day Fridays in the summer. Take a look at how changing that rule would make your organization more attractive to the startup brainiacs you want on board. The change would encourage loyalty, discourage shopping around for a friendlier job, and meld the team faster so there are no newbies chained to their desk while the senior team members get a half day off.

Your Course of Action:
Amount of work required: Most likely medium. Most of the work will come after your brainstorming sessions, when you follow up, execute, and test.
Timeframe for completion: One or more sessions.
When to execute: Your organization needs fresh products or services to stay competitive. Your culture is a bit stodgy and clunky. Team building is long overdue. Your brand is good but it's old, and people feel dated when they buy a product.
Support needed: This is best as a group effort because one person won't see everything. Keep in mind, young people tend to look at norms differently because things have changed so much over the course of their lifetimes. They can be vital for getting creative juices flowing. And their irritation factors center around speed of process, a good balance to "not throwing the baby out with the bath water" thinking.

The "real boss" this will impress: If your organization values innovation and creativity, this project can be a big hit. If your organization is slow to embrace creativity, you have the opportunity to lead innovation through a more structured process.

Benefits to organization: Helps spark innovation. Acts as the genesis for new, cutting-edge products and services. Boosts employee engagement and pride in your work.

Benefits to individual: Help yourself and your team get unstuck from old tired patterns to think vibrantly.

Cost: Free.

Potential challenges: Throwing crazy ideas out there can be risky, but that's what people need to do at times to get past limiting beliefs. It's important to be encouraging and positive during the process to ensure that it's a good experience for others. When you cultivate that type of creative environment, it will help your colleagues realize their potential for innovation. Another challenge is that senior leaders (the decision makers) might not be ready for your groundbreaking ideas. Squashing their long-standing beliefs might not happen overnight. Be prepared to present offbeat ideas by showing they are the result of a logical thought process. Video your investigation when possible. Also be ready for pushback.

Options for future enhancements: Once you use this process on one thing, you'll want to use it on another. It can be quite addictive because it's so effective. Some organizations make it a regular part of their idea-generation process.

CAREER-BOOSTING PROJECT #11: ACE NETWORKING TO BUILD YOUR "PERSONAL" BRAND

Everybody in an organization sells it. Be a face for your company at networking events. They gain great visibility—for you, the brand, the company, the department, the product, the project, and your career trajectory. Whether you are promoting products or "selling" your organizational culture, attending—or even hosting—

networking events forms connections that have big results. You could identify new recruits, form partnerships, share innovations, find new vendors, or advance direct sales. That activity becomes part of your personal brand.

A lot of higher-ups understand the power of networking but don't have the time to attend events. If you can become a go-to person for making new connections that link back to your management team, they'll recognize the above-and-beyond effort. To take this project a step further, help your company host an event. It could range from a multiday educational program in a destination city to bringing in a well-known leadership speaker or setting up a happy hour gathering at a local hot spot.

Your Course of Action

Amount of work required: Low to high. Attending networking events should just take a couple of hours every few weeks. Depending on the scale, planning and hosting events can become quite time consuming.

Timeframe for completion: If you have time this week, you could put this into practice right away. Research groups, guilds, associations, charities, and foundations that hold regular get-togethers. Look into when and where this year's array of conferences are being held so you can plan ahead. If you're hosting an event that will require guests to travel from out of town, notify them at least eight to ten months in advance. You could hold a corporate event on similar dates every year, which helps drive repeat attendance.

When to execute: You need to work on your networking skills. Your organization is struggling to stay relevant or broaden sales reach. Your competitors are active at industry events.

Support needed: Your boss's okay to attend events on behalf of your company. Approval for expenses if the event isn't free.

The "real boss" this will impress: Customers and clients. Colleagues and higher-ups who understand the importance of networking events but don't have the bandwidth to show up at them.

Benefits to organization: Meet prospects and bring in new leads for a variety of company needs. Establish and maintain a positive company presence in the industry or community.

Benefits to you: Network with people outside your organization—you never know when your team will benefit from who you know. Stay abreast of industry trends. Add to your reputation of being someone with a finger on the industry pulse, an ear to the ground, and an awareness of your company's place in the bigger picture.

Cost: Free or minimal.

Potential challenges: Bringing in new leads is a great sign that your networking efforts have created positive outcomes, but it can take time to seed those leads to pay dividends before you are recognized for your efforts. Stay motivated by keeping in mind that anyone you meet today might turn into a customer tomorrow.

Options for future enhancements: A lot of networking events accept sponsors, which is one way to help your company gain visibility. When you regularly attend events, you'll know which ones yield the best opportunities. Make it a point to meet the event organizers, who can introduce you to warm leads. Many networking events offer an educational aspect, which you can document, share with your manager and team, and apply to your organization. So stay tuned in, stay connected, and show up as often as you can. Great things can be triggered by just showing your face in the right place, at the right time, to the right person.

CAREER-BOOSTING PROJECT #12: GATHER CUSTOMER FEEDBACK—AND USE IT

Anyone who's in a client-facing role should have a feedback loop established with sales people and customer relations management.

It's vital to receive both formal and informal updates, regularly, about what clients need, how your efforts do or don't fill those needs, and their level of satisfaction with products features vis-á-vis the competition, service, ordering, troubleshooting, consultation, setup—all of it. Both praise and complaints are valuable to you and can point out areas you are blind to or haven't considered. Your consumers may feel the effects of an internal obstacle, suffer from R&D's outdated assumptions, have suggestions about improving service, or even point out company representatives who they feel are blessings or banes.

Your swift and courteous attention to servicing customer needs will impress them, your manager, and possibly other departments. You already have a variety of client comments in your head or jotted down somewhere. Organize this feedback so it isn't forgotten. Go online and check out Yelp, or type your company's name or a competitor's name followed by "sucks" into your browser—and see what comes up. Mechele makes a habit of doing this before she meets any potential new client, because it gives her a good feel for angry and frustrated buyers as she gets to know more about the client's offerings. If you can identify common themes, prioritize changes, share them with appropriate teams or departments, and continuously monitor resolutions, you will become known for being an excellent client liaison. This could lead to bigger assignments, with more responsibility or a higher level of importance, and greater overall visibility.

Your Course of Action

Amount of work required: Medium to high, depending on how much feedback you have received.

Timeframe for completion: This could be a one-off organizational project that, as feedback continues to come in, yields many ideas on an ongoing basis.

When to execute: Clients have given feedback and your organization hasn't been diligent in responding to it. You want to prioritize relationships with clients. Customer satisfaction is lower than an A-minus, which is a 90 percent positive rating. Your colleagues are working to improve products or services and need the input. Great thing to do before you are putting out fires.

Support needed: Whether you are in a client-facing role or not, you will need to collaborate with everyone who is. When you collect and organize customer feedback, you will need to assess the frequency, intensity, and level of concern that the comments convey, share it with the right people or departments, and make recommendations for how to prioritize changes.

The "real boss" this will impress: Leaders in other departments will appreciate that you are proactively—and discretely—sharing customer feedback on their departments' work. This is especially true when feedback is positive and you credit them for great work. Negative feedback should be shared judiciously with an intention to inspire positive responses.

Benefits to organization: You will gain a better understanding of customers' needs and wants, and clients will appreciate that their feedback is taken seriously and acted on. This project can also improve departmental relationships, especially if one department frequently gets criticism about work related to another department. If you can determine that what customers don't like about your software is a particular user-interface feature, or that clients are continually pushing back on a single standard term in contracts, you could clarify a whole lot. By creating a streamlined process for sharing this type of feedback, the company can truly perceive the value of changing things.

Benefits to you: Shows your attention to detail. Demonstrates your commitment to improving customer experience and benefit. Helps you gain confidence in responding to customer complaints, because they will pick up on your concerns and actions and become aware of your mediation.

Cost: Free.

Potential challenges: Some people shoot the messenger. When leaders feel pressure to make changes that are difficult or time consuming, they might not welcome hearing the feedback. That doesn't mean you shouldn't share it. Talk with your boss first if you're unsure about how to share certain feedback. He or she might have a clearer perspective on how to frame the information and whether, for political or strategic reasons, your comments should go on the back burner for a while.

Options for future enhancements: Recording customer feedback should become a regular process for anyone who receives it. Sometimes companies have technology that allows them to capture customer and competitor feedback, but employees should be able to manually enter comments they hear personally. Even a shared document on the company intranet is better than nothing. Small steps to stay organized can help your leadership team better understand customer's needs and wants and adapt to meet them.

CAREER-BOOSTING PROJECT #13: TURN PROSPECTS INTO CLIENTS FASTER

Yes, salespeople can be dynamic, charismatic, and responsive. There are a lot of soft skills that go into the role, but when you don't have the system to back you up, opportunities will fall through the cracks. You need clear ways to record your leads, schedule follow-ups, tag team with colleagues, document any contact, brainstorm need-based approaches, and share strategies that worked. Many companies would benefit from streamlined sales processes and tools. There are a variety of ways to do this.

- Create template emails for following up with leads. That

way, sales reps can copy, paste, customize a few details, and send away.

- Use software to send automated emails at specific stages in the sales process. This is known as a "drip campaign." Many email marketing platforms or CRM systems will automatically follow up with leads at any point in the sales cycle you set it to.
- Look at ways to reduce customization in proposals and contracts. While customization can make customers feel like you truly understand them and demonstrates your support, it also takes much more work and a lot longer to respond to leads with pitches or bids. Seek ways to strike the right balance.
- Create a robust library of materials that highlight what your company can do for a lead so you can save time explaining the nuances individually. For example, if you always answer the same questions on prospecting calls, create a marketing piece or a series of blog posts that share these answers. That way, you can summarize your solution with prospects over the phone and then send a document or link with more detail.

Your Course of Action

Amount of work required: Low to high.

Timeframe for completion: It depends on the strategies you implement, but the goal is to spend some time up front to save a lot of time later.

When to execute: The sales team is understaffed or too overwhelmed to pursue new leads. Salespeople are unfocused and there needs to be more consistency in the way they respond to prospects. Overpromising in the sales process and underdelivering has created issues with current clients.

Support needed: You will likely need approval from higher-ups to change proposals and contracts. Getting the sales management on your side is the best way to start.

The "real boss" this will impress: Everyone in the company benefits from increased sales. Senior leaders, your boss, and the sales and marketing teams will appreciate your work the most.

Benefits to organization: This can lead to big time-savers for the sales team and other leaders. Ensures prospects are receiving similar "performance promises" messages, regardless of the sales associate who is managing the response.

Benefits to individual: This project can be a big undertaking, and it will show off your ability and skills to manage something that affects so many people and departments.

Cost: Free.

Potential challenges: You will need to find a balance between getting your sales proposals done with few or no hitches, getting it done so that there is buy-in, and creating materials that maximize sales results. Getting support when there are many cooks in the kitchen can be difficult and require negotiation.

Options for future enhancements: Your sales process should never be static because customers' needs aren't static. You must evolve continually over time. This means keeping sales materials fresh and updated, regularly reflecting on your process, and always seeking further improvements. It could be costly but necessary, and the payoff keeps on into the future.

CAREER-BOOSTING PROJECT #14: STAY CURRENT—UPDATE YOUR WEBSITE

A website is a public face. It makes an immediate impression, and it conveys your company's style—therefore it is your most important public relations tool. The public assumes that the content is current, that the design captures the flavor of what you offer, that the tone reflects your culture. Even the font and colors share a message. So if it uses yesterday's technology, is hard to navigate, or makes people drill into it more than they have the patience to do, you need to look at its usability. And if anything has changed in the company—from the name of the CEO, to the company logo, to a new product feature, to the fact that dogs are now allowed in the office—you need to update its look or its content.

While this is hard to argue with, attending to the website commonly falls by the wayside. Sometimes it's just plain hard to agree on exactly how to update it. Maybe you don't have someone in-house who knows how to make the changes. Or you see a problem others are overlooking. Don't hesitate to take this project on, especially if you are a small business. It is a great opportunity to refresh vision, collaborate, learn new backend skills, or think outside a rut. Here are some ways to approach it.

- Is it intuitive to use?
- Is all the information accurate and navigation simple?
- Is everything current, including the colors, the content, the bios, and the external links?
- Is there anything helpful to add, like success stories or testimonials, logos of new clients, a recent case study of services, results from a scientific study, icons for the company's social media handles, links to relevant news articles, or photos from a volunteer day?
- If your company has a blog, you could write a guest post.

You can develop the content or initial plan for these changes without any knowledge of website design. It's easy to find help—just make sure you check their references and portfolio. Another way to get it done is to underwrite a class project in a local college or design school where students are assigned real-life business challenges. You could even make it a competition and award a prize for the best submission.

Your Course of Action

Amount of work required: This project is incredibly scalable. If you know enough about coding or can use backend content management to make changes yourself, simple changes could take just a few minutes. If you coordinate a revamp and work with an outside firm, the project can get as big as your ambitions for it.

Timeframe for completion: Development companies can build or totally revamp websites within days or weeks. The parts that take longer are deciding what pages you need, writing and agreeing on the content, and going through rounds of revisions to the design.

When to execute: Your website hasn't been updated in more than a year. It's starting to look and feel dated and noncompetitive. Information needs correcting. Products aren't current. Customers are having a hard time getting it to come up in searches. Clients are complaining that they can't find the information they need. Your site doesn't work well on mobile devices.

Support needed: You will need approval from higher-ups to update the website, and you will need to run content changes by various departments, the marketing team, or even the CEO. Check in with your boss about what stakeholders to include.

The "real boss" this will impress: Prospects and customers will enjoy a better user experience and benefit from accurate information. Leaders who aren't website savvy will be pleased that someone has stepped up to the plate and they don't have to manage the project themselves.

Benefits to organization: A high-quality website helps with branding, bringing in leads, and maintaining current customers. It will help your company remain competitive in the industry.

Benefits to individual: The internet isn't going away, so any knowledge you gain about websites can benefit you at any point in your career.

Cost: This project is free if you can manage updates on your own. If you outsource website development, fees range quite a bit and depend on the scope of the assignment. Offshore development work can be done for less, but it may be harder to communicate with developers who speak English as a second language. US-based companies typically charge considerably more, but they can advise on what content to include, and the project is likely to run more smoothly. Depending on the scope of updates and functionality of the site, fees can range from a few hundred dollars to the six-figure range.

Potential challenges: People are vocal with their opinions about the company website, and their opinions vary. So get advice from people who understand website best practices, trends, and user experience. You can always bring in experts to assess your site and propose what's best and why.

Options for future enhancements: Websites are not static projects—they need to be reviewed, revamped, and maintained often. It's something you could become a go-to expert on and be the center of something that is essential to your company.

CAREER-BOOSTING PROJECT #15: GET SOCIAL MEDIA SAVVY AND GET KNOWN

News outlets are not the main platforms for experts any longer. Thanks to social media, companies and individuals are turning into their own media outlets. You can use sites like Twitter, Facebook, LinkedIn, Instagram, Snapchat, Huffington Post, Google+, and Tumblr to share your own content, comment, answer questions, and help spread attention-worthy articles and messages. Being seen as an expert in your field boosts your brand recognition, brings in new clients, cultivates relationships, and affects revenue. You can use this project to help spur on your company's efforts or enhance your personal presence.

Your Course of Action

Amount of work required: This project is scalable. The more work you put in, the bigger change you will make.

Timeframe for completion: You will need to set up thorough profiles as you join each site. Take the time to really, fully understand how each platform works so that you can make the most of it. While they each work differently, they are all intuitive to use. There's a bit of a learning curve to understand the types of content that get read, shared, and liked. This is an ongoing project that will feel easier and more natural as time passes.

When to execute: You are uncomfortable using social media. The millennials in your organization are making you feel old school and out of touch. Your company doesn't have social media accounts or doesn't update them regularly. One person or department is working hard to improve social media and your support would be appreciated. You want to improve your personal branding or profile and become known as a recognized thought leader in your industry.

Support needed: You can learn a lot about best practices online. If you want to join your organization's effort, connect with the people who currently handle social media to see how they're approaching it. Even if your company has a strong social media engine running, you can still become involved. Try retweeting your company's tweets, reposting articles your company publishes on LinkedIn, following your clients, and sharing the new post on your company's blog. This promotes your personal brand and your company at the same time. If no one else is handling social media, you can become an instant go-to person if you volunteer for it.

The "real boss" this will impress: Creating content can be hard work, even if it's only 140 characters at a time. Whoever manages your social media channels will appreciate your help, not to mention HR and senior management who are aware that "social" is the new price of entry to attract high-quality staffers and potential leaders. Social media is about interaction, so when employees get involved online it makes the process easier and makes the content more thought provoking.

Benefits to organization: Improved online presence. Strengthens the organization's reputation for employing thought leaders.

Benefits to you: Social media is here to stay, so you can continue to use your newfound and evolving skills wherever your job takes you. Boosting your presence online makes you a more important player industry wide.

Cost: Free.

Potential challenges: It takes some time to get the hang of social norms on the various social media platforms. It's akin to learning a new language—it will take some practice and patience. But when you get it down, there is unlimited potential for reaching people.

Options for future enhancements: There is an endless number of things you can do to improve your social media skills and posts. As technology advances, you'll need to learn new tricks and platforms to keep up. Once you learn the basics, it's a lot easier to understand the enhancements that social media platforms roll out over time as they evolve. You can evolve with them and stay on top of trends.

CAREER-BOOSTING PROJECT #16: DO GOOD, GIVE BACK, AND THRIVE ALL-ROUND

Everyone benefits when companies make a positive impact in society. Customers care about corporate responsibility—and so do employees. So help your company take a more serious look at doing things to give back to the community and the planet. And jump into causes you care about and feel strongly driven to help, because the personal rewards are enormous. Mechele and I are passionate about helping military veterans, and we enjoy doing work that helps them find jobs and thrive in the community after they end their service. We also do a lot of work to help people who stutter. Annie Glenn, a huge supporter for the disabled and a fellow stutterer, is one of our close friends and colleagues. Both causes are dear to my heart because I identify with the challenges those individuals face. Do some self-reflecting and find a cause that is dear to your heart.

Your Course of Action

Amount of work required: Likely medium.

Timeframe for completion: It may take research to find the right nonprofit or charity to partner with, and you might be recruiting other volunteers or donors. You could attend one-time galas, sponsor annual fundraising efforts like races or concerts, form a team among coworkers to participate and seek sponsors, or simply write a check. It's up to you.

When to execute: You have a passion for helping others. You yearn to find deeper meaning in your job. You suspect your coworkers want to give back but need guidance on how and what to do.

Support needed: You will need approval to begin any philanthropic effort on your company's behalf, whether you're asking for time to work on a project, financial support, or permission to ask your coworkers to donate their time or money. When you get approval, you'll need at least a few of your coworkers to get involved to make the project a success.

The "real boss" this will impress: Helping others is admirable, and you will be respected by a wide range of people. HR will appreciate extra support in rallying behind a cause that helps the company give back.

Benefits to organization: Builds employee pride and retention. Bolsters recruiting since people are attracted to companies that give back. Contributes to a reputation for being a good, caring place to work.

Benefits to you: Feel good about your work. Build your network and meet new people in the philanthropic community. Get to know more of your colleagues. Boost your skills by organizing events or leading a group effort.

Cost: Free.

Potential challenges: It can be difficult if people don't share your passion or enthusiasm for supporting philanthropic efforts. Although "do good" work has emotional appeal, don't take it personally if people don't get on board. You might need to do some of the planning in your free time.

Options for future enhancements: If you want to give back, you can always find more to do as you watch the benefit spread.

CAREER-BOOSTING PROJECT #17: CHECK THE CULTURAL CLIMATE AND SET A BETTER TEMPERATURE

Descriptions of a company's culture can simply be monotone expressions of something that's well touted year after year. Everyone gives the same lines: We're customer focused. We work hard and play hard. We respect our employees.

Sure of that? The fact is, it's very hard to know what's going on when you're on the inside—especially as a leader. When growth makes you so desperate for new talent that you recruit for experience at the expense of character and attitude, you may find that isolationism or careerism has crept into your culture. The next time you walk through your company, physically or mentally, go a little slower and take a cultural audit.

When I was hired to take the helm of the Robert A. Becker advertising agency (now the French-owned Havas Health) in 1988, the company was sinking. It had been acquired by a British media company, and its prospects looked very dim. Once known for winning creative awards, Becker was getting pink slips from almost every one of its clients. The culture, if you could even call it that, was one of despair.

I developed a plan to reboot the agency into a client marketing partner that could think and feel like a pharma company. Having been a pharma-industry executive for the eighteen years previous, I began recruiting account people from the industry itself—people who knew advertising and PR and how to rev up a sales team and who had successful track records in how to position and drive brands. If we were going to be a one-of-a-kind marketing and sales effectiveness agency, we needed a staff that understood and had lived through what our clients were facing. It required a total culture shift.

To get the rest of the agency on board, all managers had to walk the walk. If that meant brainstorming and critiquing our clients' marketing plans unasked, we took the risk. The staff joined me for early and late-day strategy brain dumps. I wanted to model that things had sharpened up and we were gearing up for a fight for our survival. Tardiness wasn't acceptable anymore. If it meant closing people out of staff meetings because they were five minutes late, we did that. We were striving for meaningful change in every organizational crevice. And you know what? It worked. We became a lean, mean success machine. We eventually became the number two healthcare agency globally. We stuck with "Becker Values," and my alumni still do.

I can tell you from personal experience that doing a temperature check on your culture is a great way to help your organization and boost your career. If you think it's time to reengineer your culture, here are a few ideas:

- Identify behaviors consistent with your desired cultural philosophy, and reward people for these behaviors. This is a more effective way to shift culture than reprimands.

- Redefine your organization's values to capture the culture you want.
- Enlist your senior leadership team. Give everyone a mission to "think and act purpose." When the top managers of a company can agree on a culture and act as role models, change will come through fast, especially when you're reinventing the company.
- Update performance review metrics to align with your company's mission and desired culture. For example, if accountability is a priority, have this metric on the performance review and weight it to count more. Our wallpaper at Becker's Advertising office read "If it ain't great, don't do it . . . if it ain't great, don't show it."

Your Course of Action

Amount of work required: It will vary depending on the situation, but this can be a tough project.

Timeframe for completion: Ongoing. It will take extra work to get to a point where you can maintain the culture you want.

When to execute: Employees share their gripes about the company at the first opportunity. Tenured workers don't reinforce values in new hires. People seem more worried about working to get their bonuses than working because they are passionate about the company and its products. You are a senior leader or HR professional and this type of work is within your range of control.

Support needed: To make a real cultural shift, a lot of people need to support the change, especially the CEO, senior leaders, and managers. Strive for buy-in from the top. If you can't get it, this project could be incredibly hard to get off the ground. And note to self: it may be time to begin looking elsewhere.

The "real boss" this will impress: HR, the board, other company leaders.

Benefits to organization: People are happy to come to work and look forward to doing a great job. Reinforcing a great company culture accomplishes a lot more than buying a ping-pong table or serving free pizzas every Wednesday. When your culture is more clearly defined, you can hire people who express values consistent with your culture.

Benefits to individual: Take ownership in actively shaping your organization. Boost your reputation as a skilled leader.

Cost: Free.

Potential challenges: Avoid gimmicks. Ocean liners don't turn on a dime, and neither will your culture.

Options for future enhancements: Work hard consistently for change. Take frequent walks through your company. Do you like what you see and hear? Do you like the vibes? Are you proud? That's the sound of a cultural click. Keep up what you're doing to keep sailing the ship in the same direction.

CAREER-BOOSTING PROJECT #18: TRANSCEND THE SILO MINDSET TO THINK BIG

Siloing is a big problem. Barriers between departments or teams result from so many things: geographical distance, issues between managers, terse communications, personality conflicts, competition, bureaucracy, one-upping, different phases in a product cycle, or one team inheriting another team's messes. Break down those troublesome silos by learning how P&G and Amazon did it and how they impacted their success by cooperation. If you can do something to reach out that transcends this counterproductive silo effect, it will get noticed as an effort to support a bigger, whole-company outlook.

Create a project that removes barriers. Every effort to break down silos will be appreciated. This could be a multiteam effort, in which you collaborate or ask for input, or it could serve a need you clearly perceive. You could create an internal e-newsletter or contribute content to the intranet. You can and should propose an interdepartmental job swap: a product engineer could swap with a marketing associate, or a compliance officer could swap with a salesperson. Just an afternoon of job shadowing is a good place to start. These efforts help employees understand other departments, their needs, their struggles, and their talents—which promotes teamwork and productivity. It gives people a fresh look at roles and departments, which can spark new ideas for ameliorating inefficiencies, making competitive advancements, and finding new solutions to old problems.

Crest White Strips may have never been created if Procter & Gamble hadn't decided to break down departmental silos. You might think P&G had cross-departmental brainstorms all the time, but they did not, and still might not. But when the head of the oral division decided to meet with a totally different department—the tape division—they came up with the idea to combine a Crest whitening product with an adhesive. This product is now the number-one whitening product on the market.

Breaking down departmental barriers and unquestioned norms is something most leaders strive for, but it's unusual in many big manufactures to cross-fertilize between manufacturing and research or marketing and sales. If you can lead an effort to do this, you will show your own sense of priority and allegiance.

Your Course of Action
Amount of work required: Likely medium.

Timeframe for completion: Job swaps or shadowing can drive change after just a couple of hours. Build a process into the exchange for employees to reflect on what they learned and bring this knowledge back to their own departments.

Examples of situations to execute: Many employees are unaware of what is happening outside of their department. Productivity could be improved if people communicated better across the company.

Support needed: This project can require a lot of coordinating. You will need approval from your boss and higher-ups to turn this into a bigger project. If you are lower on the totem pole at your organization, you could lead this project on a smaller level in a variety of ways. Start with leading by example and illustrate with case studies, proactively share updates with other departments via email, or ask for a brief status meeting. Whenever you make communication helpful and easy, you will naturally gain others' support.

The "real boss" will this impress: Senior leaders and executives will be impressed by your ability to think big picture and come up with ways to solve challenges that affect the entire organization.

Benefits to organization: Improves teamwork, collaboration, innovation, and productivity.

Benefits to individual: Boosts your reputation as someone who brings people together.

Cost: Free.

Potential challenges: It is difficult to change the ways in which people work. When departments are accustomed to doing their own thing, how and when they want, without sharing information, it can be difficult to start a new trend. Find ways to help people understand the importance of communication and keeping others informed and involved. Another potential challenge is finding the connecting points for collaboration with people who have different goals and viewpoints than colleagues within your own department. This can feel a little uncomfortable at first, but overcoming differences is a healthy process.

I had the pleasure of interviewing Congresswoman Kathleen Rice for a lecture series at Fordham University. She told me that she bolsters her productivity by getting to know her political opponents. She said she makes a point of sitting with conservative Republicans with whom she disagrees and enjoying their company as people. Finding agreement with those colleagues is the key to getting things done, she said. Rice held up criminal justice reform as an example. Republicans and Democrats both agree that reform is needed, although for different reasons. This works to form bipartisan support.[22] You can think about relationships with different departments in the same way. Sometimes the best thing you can do is drop the roles, differing viewpoints, and various motivations and just enjoy each other.

Options for future enhancements: There are a lot of creative options for making interdepartmental communication a norm at your organization. Interdepartmental job swaps and cross-collaboration can be a big hit, and you might find that after doing it once, employees ask that it become a regular project.

MOMENTUM-BUILDING STRATEGIES

We want to close this chapter by helping bring ideas home and into your workaday reality. For every project that caught your eye, ask these questions:

- What problem do I or my company face that this project would solve?
- How immediate is the need to resolve it?
- Who would the stakeholders be?
- Who would benefit from it the most?
- How much in resources (time and money) would it require?
- Am I likely to get immediate approval and buy-in, or do I need to prepare strategically to obtain it?

Once you have answered these questions, you are ready to set your sights on success. Before you begin work on a project, read the next chapter, because there are definitely ways to do things that get overlooked and there are absolutely ways to do things that grab attention. To boost your career, you must know the difference.

4

Launch Your Impact Projects

THINGS ARE HEATING UP FOR YOU. YOU are seeing new ways forward! Now even obstacles are opportunities, because you can act to remedy them in ways that matter and get noticed. Whether you set out to build from scratch, refresh a process, expand on efforts, or reach out to others, the projects in the last chapter can work for you while you work to make positive changes.

It's time to focus on how you will implement the projects. There are ways to act that make big impressions. Don't assume you will become a hero for contributing an idea, even if it is a *very* good idea. You need to follow through on it. First, create the formal proposal that clearly demonstrates its value to your organization. Then define your step-by-step action plan to take it up the ranks, get buy-in and feedback, and gain approval on your execution plan. Last, budget the hours in the week you and others will devote to it.

Don't think that any old effort will do. You need to apply your passion, discipline, and EQ—in addition to the skillset you were hired for. We've found, again and again with thousands of people over the course of decades, that when you focus on the right things, what has until now been your "potential" can be applied and established in highly visible ways.

This chapter helps you set your sights on seven things as you launch your meaningful project and see it through. Along the way, we offer you a lot of advice and resources you can turn to. Because when you have a focused view, accurate aim, and clear intention, navigating the practicalities becomes easy. You can prioritize tasks and deal with setbacks. Use this chapter to set your sights on the right things as you take off.

SET YOUR SIGHTS TIP #1: FOCUS AND APPLY YOUR PASSION

Above all, have passion for the projects you lead. It provides the desire to keep moving forward, and is also contagious. It rallies people around you and makes your efforts visible. It will set you apart, at any level, in any team, for any project. The thing is, passion can't be faked. Don't set out to lead a project that looks good on paper but doesn't pass your gut check. As you honestly assess whether you can get 100 percent behind something, keep this in mind: passion and focus are dependent on a mindset that comes from seeing a big picture.

What does that big-picture passion result from? All kinds of things. You could be very passionate about tasks you are good at. Projects that are creative or innovative. Or you love bringing people together. Brainstorming. Inspiring other peoples' successes. Beating quotas. You might love the sense of accomplishment so much that crossing off your to-dos are high moments in your day.

It's different for everyone—the source of your passion may lie under the surface of a project. It could be found in how you do things: you enjoy puzzling over a dilemma, executing with a clear focus and sharp efficiency, taking fresh looks, or plotting strategic moves. It could be found in the ultimate outcomes: you enjoy feelings of completion, advancing your skills, seeing the benefit you bring play out, or meeting a goal. It could be found in doing things you excel at: you enjoy becoming fluent in a new coding language, moderating meetings or brainstorms, spurring on other's efforts, or making many moving parts work together.

Take out your notes from the exercise you did in chapter 1, "Your Strongest Muscles at Work." This can help you drill down to your strengths, which lay at the heart of passion. You can also check out the book by Tom Rath called *Now Discover Your Strengths*. It starts with an online self-assessment that generates your top five strengths, in order. The categories aren't the types of things you might think of on your own, so they can expand you experience of passionate engagement.

When you can identify what makes you passionate about a project, the whole effort will be boosted. It's true that some of the tasks it will require might not be your favorite things to do—so do them while focusing on a big-picture passion. Ask yourself: What does completing this task mean in the long run? Recall that it will up your chances for that raise or promotion or lateral move you crave—that it will boost your career—and you will naturally be empowered by your passion.

SET YOUR SIGHTS TIP #2: URGENCY PROPELS MOMENTUM

The quicker and more efficiently you get things done, the more you will accomplish. When you are leading an impact project, it's up to you to give it this sense of urgency. Whether you're giving yourself momentum or motivating a team, keep the benefits of completing the project high in your mind. What you lack today you could have tomorrow.

Urgency is best created when you lead by example. Set the tone and mindset for projects, and others will join it, often subconsciously. To bring this message home, here's a story of what can happen if you lag. Sarah is a millennial who worked an entry-level, business-to-business sales job at a multilevel marketing company. It was a tough job, and she was only paid through commission. The sales reps were taught that closing sales was a result of cold-calling dozens of potential customers a day. It could only be done with a sense of urgency. Sarah had it, and she was meeting her goals.

After a few months on the job, the sales reps were charged with leading all-day interviews where candidates shadowed them in the field. If the interview went well, the sales reps could hire the interviewee to join the company as a direct report. One day, Sarah had an interviewee named Jason with her when she had an unusually good morning. She closed three sales before lunch, earning over $500 in commission. Sarah usually took a fifteen-minute lunch break at a deli counter to save time, but that day she felt like celebrating. Giordano's (a famed pizza restaurant chain in Chicago) was nearby, so she suggested they eat there. It could have been quick if she hadn't agreed to order a deep-dish pizza, which took an extra thirty minutes in the oven. As they relaxed at the restaurant for more than an hour, Sarah could tell Jason thought he had just hit the jackpot with the cushiest, easiest sales job ever. Sarah told him that their morning was not typical and that she usually took a shorter lunch because every minute counted. But Sarah quickly found out that people learn by how you act, not what you say.

But Sarah liked Jason's enthusiasm for the job, so she offered him a position and he accepted. From that day forward, Jason never had one iota of urgency. When he was with Sarah in the field, he trailed along behind her at a leisurely pace. He damaged her productivity when he was with her and went even slower when he was on his own. Jason never saw as many businesses as he was supposed to in one day, which meant he didn't connect with enough prospects to maintain his quota and was never successful. After a few weeks, he had earned next to nothing in a commission-only sales job, and Sarah let him go. To her credit, she didn't put it off. Jason lacked the passion to excel and clearly had no sense of urgency or passionate execution.

Motivated direct reports follow their manager's lead. And since you are leading a project, they will follow you. If you don't hustle to make an impact every day, no one else will hustle either. As a leader, it's important to make having a sense of urgency a standard for high performance. It will motivate employees, bring clarity to tasks, and make operating on a timeline realistic and projectable. When you set an expectation for a quick working pace, trivial matters diminish in importance, priorities become clear, and it's easier to see what needs to be done. So drive productivity in ways that keep it real, doable, and quality oriented.

Whether you work with a team, outsiders, or on your own, a sense of urgency propels impact projects. By making well-timed completion of work important, you'll spread the momentum to others and build a reputation as a leader who gets things done.

SET YOUR SIGHTS TIP #3: GOALS HAPPEN ONE STEP AT A TIME

Everyone produces more when they're striving to meet specific and achievable metrics. Whatever scale your impact project is happening on, be sure to fix clear goals for it. From the beginning, motivate your team and yourself by setting and holding everyone accountable to SMART goals.

S: Specific
M: Measurable
A: Achievable
R: Realistic
T: Time-bound

These are the foundational components of goal setting. Be sure that your goals have all these qualities. You could jot this acronym down at the top of your daily goal list or on a whiteboard at every meeting with your group. Brilliant leadership expert and author Steven Covey advises "begin with the end in mind." This useful advice is one of his "Seven Habits of Highly Effective People." The most successful projects are comprised of a range of goals, rather than just a single end goal. To determine the progress points that need to be met to achieve the end goal, effective leaders work backwards to create a timeline sequence of outcomes throughout the project.

In addition to setting a larger number of smaller goals, Mechele advises it's essential for managers to overcommunicate their goals with the team. Everyone involved in a project should know what result is expected of them and what they can expect from others. Encourage your team to ask questions about the project's goals and the intended outcome they will produce. A best practice is to dedicate five to ten minutes in every meeting to asking questions, even if no one had questions at the last group meeting. Often people will lose their shyness over time, think about things in the back of their minds, or encounter new issues along the way. So when they can count on a time devoted to considering and answering questions, they are more likely to bring them up.

As a team leader, you may embrace goals, but you need to be aware—at all times—that some of your colleagues won't feel the same way. At one point or another, you will have people on your team who shy away from setting goals. It's not because they are lazy, but because they are afraid of failure. They view goals as risks. What if they can't do what they're supposed to do? Will they get in trouble or fired? Even capable people who have high self-confidence can be so risk adverse that they avoid taking on concrete commitments. If you follow the rules for creating SMART goals, your team members will be more likely to see that the purpose of goals is to help people, keep the project on track, and make them look good, rather than add unnecessary risk to their job.

For Everything You Plan to Do, Ask "By When?"

Mechele frequently works with clients at her Marketing Fire consultancy to set goals throughout their projects, and she highly recommends using a "By When?" chart. This simple, three-column chart lists all the tasks in consecutive order, identifies by name who is going to do it, and—most important—lists by when they will complete that task.

She started using this chart several years ago, and it completely changed the way her clients got things done. Clarity, accountability, and team synergy improved, and both her team and her clients became more effective by breaking projects down into smaller, manageable steps.

So start your project off on the right foot and create a "By When?" chart as soon as possible. Doing so kicks off the process of making ideas happen.

Once your team members are on the same page about goals and expectations, use the "By When" chart to have regular check-ins to discuss progress and determine whether everyone is on track. For example, if the sales team is supposed to bring in five hundred new accounts in six months and they've only brought in fifty after one month, there needs to be an open discussion about getting off track, as well as possible solutions. When teams are veering away from the target or falling short of it, the signs are usually there long before the deadline.

Since you will be having progress check-ins routinely, it will be easy to keep superiors and stakeholders abreast of your progress on a regular basis as well. If you're using a "By When?" chart, all you need to do is mark when tasks are completed. By using a document-sharing resource like your company intranet or Google Docs, superiors and stakeholders will be able to check your progress at their convenience—a best practice for transparency. Another good strategy is to ask these important individuals at the onset of the project how frequently they would like to receive updates. You will find that keeping superiors apprised of your progress adds another layer of trust and accountability—and overall visibility. Let them watch you perform and see that "potential" get to work.

SET YOUR SIGHTS TIP #4: TIMELINES GET THINGS DONE

Keep to a timeline. Always. It is essential to any endeavor. You can spearhead a groundbreaking project that beautifully shows off your intelligence and skills, but if it's behind schedule, it might do more harm to your reputation than good. At any company, in any industry, things will start to fall apart if people don't finish tasks on time or in an A+ manner. Any boss knows this. In fact, every manager or team leader has probably experienced numerous situations when someone let him or her down by not following through on due dates and superior outcomes. It puts bosses in hot water with their boss, or they have to take on the stress of busting their butts to pick up the slack.

Being late is such a big problem that we want to tell you more about the negative effects to encourage you to stay on target. Being late compromises trust. Even if it doesn't impact the overall outcome of your project, it makes people wonder if they can rely on you. This is absolutely not the way you want your boss or other senior leaders to think about you. When you become one of those "unreliable" colleagues, your chances for advancement come to a screeching halt. Nothing is worse than having to nag people to get things done. It becomes so tiresome in the workplace that it drains energy and morale from people on both ends. That's why it's essential that you consider a timeline a promise and that you start parting ways with your "C" players.

Don't get us wrong—managing a complex project and staying on track is no easy task. That's why there are whole schools of thought dedicated to project management. One of our personal favorites is Six Sigma. Developed by Larry Bossidy, former president of Honeywell, Six Sigma has become a standard for keeping a large number of people organized, focused, and, importantly, meeting their deadlines. You can become trained in the Six Sigma process to help manage projects, and there is a lot of great information available online as well. The idea is for your whole team to follow the progress on the project every single week for an hour. This simple strategy does wonders for keeping projects on time and your team members connected and engaged so the outcomes you agreed on are delivered as promised. Follow-through makes an impact, and Six Sigma is a great strategy for deadline management.

One of the most challenging aspects of keeping a project on track has nothing to do with the project itself. The real battle often lies in the competing priorities that crop up and threaten to suck time away from your impact project. You will never be able to control all the things that threaten to derail your concentration and progress, but you can control how you respond to them. First and foremost, you shouldn't be surprised. Your company is busy. That's why they employ you. If you want to be an impact leader, you must anticipate disruptions and prepare to handle them appropriately. When clients are asking you for help, your coworkers are emailing you with questions, and your direct reports need extra support, it can feel like you're being pulled in a hundred directions at once. When this happens, it's important to stay calm and think critically instead of automatically putting out fires—one after the other—until it's five o'clock and you've accomplished nothing important.

A straightforward way of staying on track is to work on the most important things first. This might sound like a no-brainer, but it's shocking how many people don't follow this bit of common sense. When you come into the office in the morning, look at your "things to do" list first thing and focus on #1—the most important task. Work on the most important task first and don't allow yourself to be distracted. When you aren't sure how to prioritize your tasks, talk to your boss and other stakeholders in the projects. It's possible that a timeline has more wiggle room than you were originally led to believe, or a colleague can step in and take something off your plate. And if you're working with people who have different priorities or don't agree with stated outcomes or the sequencing to complete tasks, one secret to success is to put these "conflict owners" into a meeting with the instruction that they need to think outside of the box, get to a resolution, and supply a "By when?" date. Then step away and let them get to work.

Do your best not to allow distractions and disruptions to alter your impact project's timeline. If you don't take deadlines and goals seriously for the projects you lead, it affects your team members' mindsets and diminishes the importance of your projects overall. If another pressing priority comes up, you may need to be agile and adjust and arrange your own "conflict owner" meeting, but that clearly is a last resort.

Recognize that sometimes certain aspects of your project won't go according to plan. As much as you and your team try to stay on schedule, you might need to adjust the timelines created at the beginning of your project. When this is unavoidable, make sure everyone involved with the project understands the situation as early as possible. Keep superiors and team informed and get their agreement that the changes to the timeline are necessary. This is much better than pulling out suddenly at the last minute.

Although it may seem like a lot of pressure to follow a set timeline, it's better to consider it an opportunity to impress your colleagues from top to bottom. When you deliver early—even a little early with a great piece of work —you come alive for your boss. You are now a stress reliever, which is the kind of thing that sticks in peoples' memories. By finishing ahead of schedule, you are ulti-mately helping in a variety of ways: efficiency can save money in the budget and the company stays ahead of the curve. As you are developing a project, there might be one or two competitors that are doing the same thing. This happens all the time in business, and it is terribly important that you work quickly to outflank them and meet important deadlines. Being on time is great, but being early is even better.

SET YOUR SIGHTS TIP #5: TEAM SYNERGY IS YOUR FUEL SUPPLY

To be collaborative, you need "people management" skills. While this can be one of the hardest aspects of leading a project, it can also fuel the effort with ideas and enthusiasms from a diverse group of people. There are so many interpersonal dynamics in the workplace that affect how employees feel about one another and work together: Lisa is overeager to impress, Brad's usually behind schedule, and Jackie tries to take credit for other people's ideas. Don't let style differences crumble a project through disengage-ment, low productivity, or lagging quality. While it isn't your job to make everyone become best friends, you do have the responsi-bility—and the opportunity—to uphold a positive, team-oriented environment.

Doing this is about more than merely "liking" each other: it's about admiration and respect and getting the best out of people. The basis of team synergy is seeing the best in everyone. Identify what they're good at and what they contribute—and focus on get-ting the best of that. Lisa also makes above-and-beyond efforts to get things done right. Brad comes up with very creative solutions to the problems he faces. And Jackie can take any assignment and run with it. You can motivate and empower your team by taking the philosophical approach that it's not "me against you" or "my way versus your way"—it's *us versus the challenge*.

Open communication is always a good policy for fostering a collaborative culture. Make it known that if anyone has concerns about the project, their role, the process, or a nitty-gritty detail they're concerned about, you welcome a one-on-one conversation. Then the two of you can determine how the issue can be addressed and whether it needs to be raised with the team or not. Especially if it's an interpersonal dynamic issue, avoid public disparagement of any kind. It negatively pays you back a hundred ways. Contrary to what some managers think, embarrassing people does not make them work harder or become more loyal to you or your cause. It doesn't motivate the people who witness the public disparagement either. When your direct reports see you give negative feedback to a colleague in a meeting or on a group email chain, they will wonder when you'll do the same thing to them. This erodes trust, team synergy, and reputation.

Although it's smart to avoid public confrontations with people who are somehow compromising an effort, that doesn't mean you can ignore the issue. Negativity can quickly damage morale and set a bad precedent, so you may need to take immediate action to rectify the situation. Brief, one-on-one meetings can build transparency, help sweep away small rule breaks, or ease discord. (And if you are the one who's been too overbearing with a colleague, do not hesitate to apologize.) People are generally reasonable once problems are brought to their attention through clear, direct, and kind feedback.

If you are working with direct reports on this project, you know how hard it can be to let people go or move them to a different role, but sometimes these hires just aren't the right fit. This often becomes obvious when your group is pivoting to apply a new approach or to fix a problem, and someone just can't get on board with evolving plans. It can also be obvious when people are disengaged in meetings: checking their phones or working on other things. When they lack the passion to make things happen, they can slow your whole effort down with the weight of their drag.

Acting quickly on hiring mistakes and moving on nonproductive players helps team synergy survive. If your direct reports can't get on board or won't productively collaborate with the rest of the team, consider if it's time to part ways . . . and do it.

If the person compromising your team's synergy isn't a direct report, you can disinvite him or her from the project. One approach Mechele coaches is to privately meet with the offender, keep it light in tone, but get around to the problem at hand. Ask the person if he can see some logical ways to fix the problem. If none suit the situation, state you want to agree to disagree and that regrettably you think he might function more productively in a different situation. Sooner than later is the best—and least harmful—time for a separation from the team. Don't be surprised if you note some relief on all parts. No one enjoys working amid conflict. In removing someone, your job is to send him on his way as undamaged as possible but out of your team's hair.

SET YOUR SIGHTS #6: OTHERS' PERSPECTIVES BRING SURPRISING BOOSTS

People are hardwired to view the world in different ways, which impacts how they react in various situations. This is evident in behavioral assessments like Myers-Briggs Type Indicator or DiSC® Profiles. Rather than seeing it as a challenge to work with people who are different from you, view it as an opportunity. On the MBTI index, you see that we are not most compatible with people who share our same type—instead we work best with people who see the world a little differently. There's a lot of truth to the old adage that opposites attract. Mechele recommends using the DiSC Workplace Test to determine the ways in which people prefer to work. When you know your own work style and how you interact with others, it can help you build a more cohesive team.

Lesley Thorne is an assistant professor at New York's Stony Brook University, and her passion lies in research. She recently collaborated with a colleague to write an article about a research study, and the pair didn't see eye to eye at first. Lesley always began her writing process by reviewing other articles and studies. Her partner always focused on the visuals first: charts, graphs, and photos. He pushed Lesley to view the story through visuals, which seemed like an odd approach to her at first. When she gave her partner's bent a chance, she was amazed by how it transformed her perspective on what was possible. She had never considered that readers are often most drawn to visuals in a magazine, and that many only read the articles with interesting photos or graphs. By building the article around the visuals, Lesley and her partner came up with an insightful piece they were really proud of writing. She said frankly that she had learned something valuable that she'll use far into the future.

You might not agree with a differing perspective when you first hear it, but don't dismiss it—once you start to explore the thinking behind it, you may realize it's a stroke of genius. The fact is that it's detrimental if everyone on your team views the world in the same way. All of you would overlook the same errors in your thought process and sadly miss opportunities to make your project outcome even better. Homogenous teams tend to have trouble accepting a new member who thinks differently than the group. The new person's perspective is often not welcomed. This is a problem for upholding a positive culture, but it's also a problem for leaders who are judged by helping their team expand, both in terms of people and ideas.

When a team sees eye to eye on virtually every issue, a good strategy is to bring in outside people or consultants to have your team become more expansive in terms of ideas and thoughts. This is often a smart strategy to drive innovation even when a team's ideas haven't become homogenous. These "outsiders" might end up having such good ideas that it transforms the project and suddenly there is a new rocket ship right in the middle of an idea that was chugging along. It's a very good sign when a team can accept these new ideas, pivot, and be proud of their progress.

Remind yourself of this when you are choosing people to help with your projects. Yes, you want to get along easily with your team members, but you don't want them to be too much like you. If you feel low compatibility with another team member, instead of avoiding that person, make a better effort to get to know him or her. That might sound uncomfortable, but it's a valuable investment of relatively little time. It can be accomplished over coffee, an after-work drink, or a walk, and it has an immeasurable payoff if it results in being more comfortable working with that person over months or even years down the road. My first move is to go to Google or LinkedIn to find out more about my colleague's background. You learn a lot from a few minutes on these sites that can assist you in creating an emotional connection.

As you lead your impact projects, make sure you keep an open mind and proactively ask for others' perspectives. Especially when you are doing big-idea brainstorming, we advocate inviting colleagues from other functions in your organization, or even guests from other businesses, to join with you and inject some fresh thoughts. If you consider the world today, our culture is changing more rapidly than ever before, largely thanks to our open-minded millennials. Millennials seem to be more keenly aware of the value of others' perspectives than other generations were at a young age. Millennials are particularly well-versed in considering different perspectives and trying them on for size. They are helping show older generations that you don't have to believe the exact same thing as other people, and you can still be tolerant and respectful of their ideas. In the Becker days, to heat up idea sharing among the entire organization, I started a "reverse mentorship" activity. Any of my reports who were over fifty partnered with a millennial for co-coaching: the millennials tutored in digital marketing, cool eating spots in town, great apps, and collaboration skills, and the older colleagues taught corporate gamesmanship, positively influencing sticky situations, and goal communication. This helpful strategy is done at many corporations today, because it builds relationships, transfers knowledge, and, perhaps more importantly, helps employees consider their coworkers' perspectives.

Making an impact is always about inviting the best to come out in the people around you, be they coworkers, direct reports, clients, or superiors. When you cultivate an environment where people feel comfortable sharing their ideas, you'll encourage everyone to bring their best to your project. By taking the time to learn about your colleagues and ask for their input, you'll be surprised by the creative and insightful suggestions they give you to make your project even better. You may come up with an idea and someone raises her hand and says, "And . . ." not "But." When this happens, you know you're doing something right. As the project evolves, continue to listen and embed your colleagues' best ideas into your work.

As you lead a new project, you must be aware that it isn't just the coworkers on your project who may have different perspective. Stakeholders are perceiving your success from different angles, and those angles are always evolving. Try to step outside of your own perspective and consider how your boss, her boss, direct reports, your peers, key customers, and, whenever possible, competitors view how you've managed your project. This isn't difficult—all you have to do is ask. In the case of competitors, ask friends and customers if there's any buzz from your rivals. If you can get feedback during the project, what you learn will help you adjust and make better decisions, ultimately leading to better results.

SET YOUR SIGHTS TIP #7: KNOWING WHEN TO FOLD KEEPS THE JOURNEY REAL

History books gloss over some aspects of the past, especially brutal military defeats. Some former military leaders were so headstrong that they thought their troops could prevail in any situation, regardless of being outnumbered, suffering from lack of proper supplies, or pure exhaustion. Instead of retreating, they initiated a new battle they had very little hope of winning. They failed to see the truth that they could not win at this juncture. No one wants to die fighting a pointless battle that a leader has gambled on and lost. As a project leader, you can learn a lot from the history that some nations would like to forget.

True leaders aren't afraid to admit when they've made a mistake. Rather than worrying about it ruining their reputation, they choose accountability. Rule #1 of crisis management is: own up ASAP. It's a smart move, especially because people tend to admire leaders who openly admit to a goof. It's not unusual for projects to be halted because they aren't working out as planned, or because new information shows the project isn't the best path forward, or because a competitor has outflanked them. When this happens, it's best to close out the project efficiently and quickly and move on to something that will create more value.

I had to fold a big project I thought was going to be a hit but that ended up coming up short. I was running a global advertising agency when I had the opportunity to start an internal consulting group that would advise our clients. Since some clients were already paying big bucks for consulting, the thinking was we could increase our service offerings and land the business they were giving to other firms. I thought, "Wow! What an opportunity to make an impact at my company!" I talked with my colleagues, and I got a lot of talented people on board to help. But the problem was that we didn't truly understand the business model of consulting. Many clients were getting consulting support through well-established, heavy-hitting consulting firms, and we underestimated how hard it would be for a new consulting group to earn that type of business. Even though we had extremely intelligent people on our internal consulting team, we could not realistically compete with industry-leading consulting firms to take away their current clients. When we became more fully apprised of how difficult this market was to break into, it was time to fold—so that's what we did.

Part of being an impact leader is recognizing when you've hit a dead end or a stop sign. New information might show your initial plan is no longer logical, that the returns won't be as high as originally thought, or it has become logistically unachievable. When this happens, folding your project is the best option for the team and the company. Don't be afraid to adapt to changing situations. Good leaders must be able to engineer change, help their team get through it, and get on to something else. Don't make it an ego battle or argue robustly for the wrong reasons. Heeding and facing the logical, unvarnished truth can actually create loyalty in your team, garner respect, reduce fear of failure, and result in winning support for your future projects. Time is so short today that being able to hop off one project and onto another is one thing you're being judged on. It's always about moving forward.

MOMENTUM-BUILDING STRATEGIES

Following these best practices will change the way you get things done. We consider these seven strategies to be the ingredients in the secret sauce of any leader's success. So set your sights on them. If more leaders today followed these simple steps, the business world would be totally different. The vast majority of companies are failing; it's just the reality in today's marketplace. Most companies will never make it because a lot of people start businesses without ever considering a good number of the suggestions in this chapter. They don't have a timeline, they don't set clear goals, they don't preserve team synergy. So what happens to their big idea? It fails. If the execution on any of these factors is subpar, the chances of achieving success drop significantly. When the ball is dropped on multiple factors, it just isn't going to work out.

This is why this chapter is so important. Now that you know what many business leaders miss, you have a clear competitive edge. Keep setting your sights on these seven things as you go about any aspect of your job, and especially on the efforts that will make meaningful impacts to boost your career.

- Find what makes you passionate about any project and use that passion to create an impact.
- A sense of urgency gets things done.
- When you know where you're headed, you know what to do to get there. So set SMART goals for the destination.
- Meeting timelines is essential to getting things done and building a stellar reputation as someone people want to work with and learn from.
- Appreciation and respect build team synergy.
- Make the most of others' perspectives to expand your own approach.
- Keep things real and keep the outcome positive, because sometimes the best thing to do is to fold an endeavor.

5

Get Beyond Your
Current Atmosphere

ANY PROJECT CAN BE DONE SUCCESSFULLY. ANY effort can make a positive impact on the company. But it will only boost your career if you get attention for it. And the more attention you get, the further you'll go.

We like to think of this as your "thrusting power." Just like when a rocket is launched into space, how far you go depends on it. You can successfully launch a project and simply become suborbital—briefly entering space and then returning to earth. This is when you get a nice pat on the back for being a good employee. Your success might be logged as a positive contribution on your annual review, but it remains viewed as part of your regular duties. Things stay the same; and we wouldn't be surprised if this isn't the biggest cause of your conundrum, your angst, and your frustration. So this moment—after you've completed your project and achieved your results—is incredibly important.

When you have generated the thrust to reach an altitude that's high enough, you become orbital—properly positioned for staying in space, in motion around the earth. You could be promoted to supervisor or team lead or given a raise for your current position. What makes the difference is how you deliver your results. You need to do it in a way that maximizes visibility.

So deliver the results in ways that make big impressions; how you do that could be even more important than what you accomplished. An engaging wrap-up narrative will bring many gains from bosses and coworkers. A bad narrative—even when the outcome was achieved—can damage a reputation, stall a career, and make everyone's effort feel like a waste. This is the crucial moment when you break earth's atmosphere and enter space; it's bumpy and takes tremendous command. If you can tell a great success story using the nine thrusting powers we share in this chapter, you won't merely poke through only to fall back. You'll ignite new fuel sources, get noticed, and stay up there.

THRUSTING POWER #1: PREPARE YOUR STORY TO SELL IT BIG

Get your narrative clear before you share your results with others. Your story needs to be—and will be—entirely factual. At the same time, prepare it so you can be smart about how you tell it. You've probably heard the saying "everyone works in sales." No matter what line of work you're in, you're "selling" your ideas to others. To get your thrusting power up, you must be able to sell the results. Mapping the journey from start to finish will make your delivery sharp and succinct.

Create a Hindsight Map
Do an analysis and write everything down. If you worked on the project with a team, do this as a group exercise. Be sure to include these steps:
- Analyze all stages of the project: What need did your project meet? What problem did you solve? What were your obstacles? What went well? What didn't go as well as you hoped?
- Recognize the lesser successes along the way: Aside from the result you were after, were there ancillary benefits to

the project? Did it position your team to have greater success in the future? Did you establish and expand relationships? Did you discover new idea-generating or problem-solving processes?

- Recall what was working against you. If you forget about challenges you faced or fail to make others aware of them, your results may seem less significant. Lessons learned are treasured data. So write down what you had to overcome.
- Identify any negative outcomes. If you try to hide them, your boss could pick up on them independently, which would be bad news because he would be left to form his own perceptions. Tackle these head-on and include them in your results.

If you do your analysis and find that you lack substantial evidence of your results, do more research. For example, you developed a new system for organizing client information. If you aren't hearing people comment on how helpful this new system is, ask colleagues whether your efforts have been useful. Not only will you get valuable feedback on your work, you'll also demonstrate that you are concerned enough to ask whether your efforts hit the mark. Sometimes it takes time to gauge the outcomes of your work. You can start recording and analyzing results, but don't jump the gun and promise what's not demonstrable yet. A timely summary may be called for, but make it clear that you can only share preliminary results until more data is available.

Armed with all this analysis, write your wrap-up narrative down as a PAR story: Problem→Action→Result. Create a page for every challenge you tackled or faced along the way. List all the actions you took, and then highlight the result. This is an extremely effective way to present your abilities, because it focuses in on the most important aspects of the project. Rehearse your PAR story diligently so that it shares your unique competency in addition to your contribution.

Once you have the pieces in place for your story, think about all the bits of information you could include to spice things up and keep your audience engaged. Could you include short clips of consumer interviews or videos of your product in action? What about expert testimony, illustrations that show the potential impact of your project, or a few colorful charts? If you feel your creativity waning, consult the Internet for inspiration. There are plenty of sample presentations online, as well as resources for stock photos, videos, and music. These "extras" aren't just fluff. They help your audience engage emotionally and respond positively to both you and your project—but mostly to you.

THRUSTING POWER #2: USE METRICS TO MAKE IMPACT TANGIBLE

Analytics are incredibly effective. Numbers make things tangible and real. And sharing them helps people understand, perceive, and appreciate your work. So quantify the results of your impact projects whenever possible. Just do it in a way that puts color into your story: "Since revamping our sales materials, we've closed 17 percent more leads, which will increase our revenue this year by an estimated $450,000." That's a meaningful impact, and framing your effort that way will guarantee attention. Production, manufacturing, marketing, and sales are great departments to go to for numerical metrics. If quantifying results is not your strong suit, get help from an analytical team member until you sharpen your skills.

Some impact projects loan themselves to metrics, but not all projects have quantifiable results. Sometimes changes are qualitative in nature. This doesn't mean you can't use metrics. Qualitative metrics simply show changes between the "before" and the "after." To identify metrics from a qualitative project, ask yourself why you took on the project. Somewhere in your head, you had a metric.

For example, maybe you noticed that no one at your office socialized with one another. That's an implied metric. It isn't mathematical, but it's a metric that serves as your baseline. If you created an employee group that helped people get to know one another, your project may have moved the needle on improving company culture, employee engagement, recruitment, and employees' commitment to stay at the organization. All of these outcomes are complex and thus difficult to measure, but not impossible. Take a close look at what has changed: there's small talk happening in the breakroom now; people smile at each other in passing; they go out to lunch together instead of eating alone at their desk. Those are real changes that make an impact.

To support your qualitative observations, ask team and nonteam members to share feedback about their observations and experiences. Do they think comradery or teamwork has improved? Do they feel less stressed throughout the day because they take lunch or short breaks to socialize or hit the company's fitness center for an hour? Can they give you an example or share an anecdote— and would they let you record them? Do they feel more likely to recommend the company to a friend or family member as a good place to work? You can share this feedback as qualitative, or even create quantitative, results: "Of the people who participated in the employee group, 60 percent said they think teamwork has improved as a result."

THRUSTING POWER #3: PREPARE SECRET
SUCCESS NARRATIVES TO MOTIVATE YOU

Even when your impact project doesn't have a definitive endpoint that requires a wrap-up and debrief with stakeholders, prepare your own success narrative. Many self-improvement projects fall under the "informal" category. Your boss might not know what you've been working on to boost your advancement prospects. He or she might not need to know: it would be awkward to deliver a formal presentation to show how much more professional, organized, or educated you have recently become. In the following paragraphs, we offer strategies for beneficially sharing your results. Follow these steps even if you aren't planning on announcing your progress to anyone. Doing so will help you become motivated in your informal project, assist or even propel any small talk about it, and help you perceive the value of your efforts. You'll also commit your accomplishments to memory so you can draw on them when it matters most, whether at a job interview five years from now or when you're coaching a mentee who reminds you of your younger and less-experienced self. It shows self-awareness to notice when personal improvement is needed, and taking steps privately is certainly admirable. Do not sell yourself short—create a secret success story and add it to your personal branding profile.

You could also think about how you can demonstrate these improvements through actions. Prepare for and then do something that will let your new skills shine: offer to announce an award at a big event; share the fact that a social media post got a hundred likes; mention that you met with an industry influencer. Any way you can show that you are stepping outside your comfort zone into new, expansive territory shows you are engaged, you are actively bettering yourself, and you believe in yourself and want to exercise your new muscle. This says a lot about you as a person and gains respect.

When your boss notices your progress, he or she may bring it up at some point, whether during a casual conversation or in a performance review. When this happens, be ready to speak confidently about your efforts. If no one mentions the improvements generated by your informal projects, don't assume they went unnoticed. I struggled for years to defeat my stammer, and my hard work paid off. I made a lot of progress improving my speech when I was working for one company in particular, but I didn't call a meeting to announce it to my boss. I didn't bring it up at all. I was confident my boss noticed my progress through my performance, despite the fact that he never thought it necessary to acknowledge. This is often the case for self-improvement work. Remember, a pat on the back can be nice, but you don't always need it from others. Offer yourself your own.

THRUSTING POWER #4: KNOW YOUR AUDIENCES AND MAKE YOUR STORY MEET THEIR NEEDS

One size doesn't fit all. Consider who's sitting there, listening to you. Is it your superiors? Direct reports? Clients? Then tailor your communication to resonate with them. Think about them as individuals—what do they care about? Identify that and shape your presentation around it. For example, your boss's highest priority is getting a pipeline of qualified job applicants so she can hire new talent ASAP. If your philanthropy project connected you with a few strong job candidates who have impressive resumes and glowing references, describe how you got to know them.

Keep in mind that most professionals are crunched for time. And some get invited to so many meetings that there is little time for anything else. So a thirty-minute PowerPoint presentation is likely much more than what your audience needs or wants. People appreciate it when you value their time, and you can always tell your story more concisely than you originally thought. The best communicators keep it short and impactful. They know giving a client back some time is part of the "win."

If your company keeps past PowerPoint decks on file, do some research and see what types of presentations have worked well for people previously. If you can find presentations that were created by the people you will be presenting to, that will give you great insight on how they think. For example, if your boss's presentations contain a lot of metrics, she might place a high value on backing up results with data. Consider mirroring that style in your own presentation.

Make it easy for your audience to share your results with others. The further your success story can go, the better. When presenting to your boss, think about how she would share it with her boss and make it easy for her. Don't assume she can remember all the details of your project or that she even wants to commit those details to memory. Instead, proactively create a summary version of your PowerPoint: a PAR story with some details in a slick-looking slide deck that's brief, easy to read, and to the point. Mechele's old boss used to say, "Be brief, be bright, be gone!" Your boss will appreciate your foresight in creating materials to communicate with two different audiences.

Also consider adjusting your messaging based on behavior or personality types. People perceive information in very different ways, and you will have the most success communicating with different types of people when you become attuned to how they view the world. Think back to your MBTI or DiSC research, and see if you can identify the behavioral types of your real bosses. Is your CEO a High D who likes information to be quick and direct? Or maybe your manager is a High C who is very analytical and will want you to cover the details. A client may be a High I who places a lot of weight on personal relationships when making business decisions. All of these behavioral types are motivated by different things, which means your results will resonate best when you present them in ways that accommodate the listener's processing style.

It can be difficult to cater to different personality types when presenting to a group, but not impossible. For example, if you're presenting in person, keep your presentation concise and your slides clean, but bring handouts with all the background information for people to reference if they want. If you present on a conference call or webinar, make sure people get more information emailed to them. You want to avoid information overload, but you should always have more information ready for those who want it.

THRUSTING POWER #5: GET FEEDBACK AND PRACTICE YOUR DELIVERY

Before sharing results with your most important stakeholders (your real bosses), get another perspective from astute people you trust. Share your interpretations of results with close colleagues, customers, mentors, or friends. If you will ultimately be presenting to higher-ups, start by bouncing ideas off your immediate superior. Remember, your supervisor is on your side. Chances are, your presentation will go much smoother if you let her critique it first. (You don't ever want to surprise her in a meeting with her superiors present.)

If you get negative feedback, stay cool, be open, and avoid a gloomy reaction. Ask clarifying questions that help you get to the root of what isn't resonating in your story. Try to take a step back from the project and listen objectively. Constructive criticism is a gift because it gives you the opportunity to refine your delivery and make improvements before the formal presentation.

If you're presenting results to a boss, to a senior leader, or in any formal situation, do at least one dry run. You never want to wing it. I always coach my direct reports and help them practice before they give a presentation to the board or executive committee. I also practice interviewing skills with my MBA students at Fordham. I talk with them about how to look, speak, keep eye contact, shake hands, dress, and answer questions, because all of that matters. It matters for making a first impression and getting a job, but it's just as important after you get the job. Whenever you get an opportunity to be in front of your boss, it's like another audition. You are essentially interviewing to move forward at the company, which is something that deserves practice.

The first thing many people realize when they do a dry run is that they are talking too fast. The slower you speak, the smarter you sound. Think about how slowly former President Barack Obama speaks. You can understand every word because he isn't rushing. His slow pace of speech makes him seem thoughtful and confident. Now think about the opposite—maybe a quick-talking, annoying salesperson. People tend to talk fast when they are nervous, lying, unsure, or trying to distract their audience from the last thing they said. Certainly, that's not what you want to sound like when you are presenting your results. After you practice your careful delivery and successfully slow down your pace, make sure you practice one more time the morning of the presentation. Look at yourself in the mirror, smile, and start talking. Think of it this way: you're the doctor and your audience is the patient. You bring news of a cure. Slow down and let your audience know!

Sometimes people maintain good eye contact at the beginning of a presentation but lose steam partway through. Looking people in the eye is not only important for trust, it helps build an emotional connection. You must be excited to tell *this* person your results. If presenting to a group, be sure you make good eye contact with the entire group. You don't always know who the decision makers will be.

You can't walk in tired and droopy and think people should be thanking you for your work. They won't. You may have done a great job, but if you aren't polished, it will be harder for people to tell. Don't limit your opportunities because you aren't prepared to give a good impression when you share your results. Here's what I tell my MBA students: walk into a meeting with confidence, maintain eye contact, give a firm handshake if the situation calls for it, and keep that slight "Bill Clinton" smile on their face. When they sit down, their spine should be pressed into the back of the chair with good, but relaxed, posture. I tell them not to cross their legs because it opens the door for wardrobe malfunctions. For women, skirts can scrunch up too high for the workplace, and for men, unshined shoes and falling-down socks can look unprofessional. Better to cross the feet at the ankles or not cross them at all.

My students sometimes chuckle when I get so specific about my advice on what to do and wear to impress. But from my many years of experience in corporate environments, I know that while senior executives might not look like fashionistas themselves, that doesn't mean they are blind to body language and attire faux pas.

THRUSTING POWER #6: PUSHBACK WILL HAPPEN— BE READY TO FACE IT

Depending on the scope of your project, it can be smart to ask your boss to which leaders you should send a small synopsis before presenting the full results. Let these select individuals peek under the hood before the meeting. It's a smart strategic move, because it enables people to raise issues or get amplification before the meeting instead of putting you on the spot. Chances are, you will have greater success in responding to concerns when you have more time to reflect on them and do additional research.

When you present your results, know that people will have questions that might feel like criticism. Here's one: "These sales figures seem impressive, but we usually see an uptick in sales after a competitor goes through a merger. Are you sure your results aren't being skewed by ABC Widget's recent acquisition?" You must make questions feel welcomed, even if they make you a little uneasy. When you get a tough question, take a breath and think through the answer for a minute before opening your mouth. This will help you look thoughtful as well as help prevent you from going on the offensive—and from going on the defensive. If you don't know the answer, by all means, don't make it up! Thank the person for raising the question and say you will get the answer for her or him and report back ASAP.

As you can see, anticipating questions is in your best interest because it produces a smoother presentation. One key goal in analyzing your project's results is to make sure you're learning from your company's history. When you share recommendations with leadership, sometimes you will hear, "No, we've tried that before and it didn't work." Instead of being blindsided, you can say, "Yes, it's true there are similarities with these two projects, but we've created a new strategy and tactical plan." There will always be people who like to play devil's advocate, so be ready for their annoying negativity. Mechele recommends regaining control of the meeting by asking a devil's advocate to briefly explain why a past project he is criticizing didn't work. This can be a good way to quickly highlight the key differences in your project and get past those issues.

THRUSTING POWER #7: SPREAD THE CREDIT AND GO HIGHER WITH HUMILITY

If a leader takes all the credit for whatever success the department or division achieves, it is frustrating to colleagues and damages workplace culture. Former ACS CEO Jeff Rich dubs these types of poorly trained managers "shade trees." He calls them by that wonderfully descriptive title because "They're huge. They soak up all the sunshine coming down on their organization, and they don't let any of the credit go below them." He adds, "Relying on just financial compensation to grow loyalty isn't enough. People have the need to be recognized in other ways."[23]

People with genuinely high self-esteem don't have to take a lot of credit. They give credit to the people around them. And you know what? People love them for that. When I was chairman of Robert A. Becker, now Havas Health, it was always about the great work people did. At town hall meetings, I spoke about getting the best out of people. I never spoke about the great work I did. If I wanted to talk about my work, it was always through the lens of what other people did to contribute. I believed in their work just as much as my own. This is the mentality I was taught, and you need to have it to lead.

Who Gets Kudos? Everyone.

Don't leave anyone out when you are spreading the credit around. Use this exercise to recall everyone who contributed to the project, even the assistant who ordered your dinners in when you were working late. Because if you overlook some-one, you are doing the same disservice you have suffered from in the past. You know that it breeds harm to relationships and motivation. So take out some paper, write down every-one's name, and identify their contribution. Use this list to send thank-you emails and notes, or to plan your presentation acknowledgments. Because you know that assistant went out of his way to get you the best curry in town.

It's not uncommon for egomaniacs to rise through the cor-porate ranks, but they make work very unpleasant for the peo-ple around them. So when senior leaders experience success and stay humble, it's often an ironic truth that they end up getting even more recognition. General Motor's CEO Mary Barra took over when the company was experiencing its darkest days—the aftermath of safety scandals, bankruptcy, and a reputation melt-down. Barra has made a lot of progress turning things around, including stubborn stock prices. Insiders say it's because of her collaborative work style and "controlled ego that lets others have the limelight."[24] No doubt, this contributed to her winning the number one spot on *Fortune* magazine's list of Most Powerful Women 2016.

Barra is experiencing great success, and you can learn a lot about her from what she did before she became CEO. Barra had worked at GM her entire career, but that didn't make her a shoo-in. She got the job because people liked and admired her. She wasn't busy tooting her own ego horn. She was getting things done and getting the best out of her people. That's what making an impact and boosting your career is all about.

When you share your results from your impact project, don't ever hesitate to admit you were wrong about something. Proactively bring up what you could have done better before others may point it out to you. Explain what you learned from your mistakes. If you worked with a group, mention and congratulate your people. That's how you build your team. As you build your reputation for being a leader who respects and appreciates others, and chooses to give accolades to colleagues rather than taking the credit, you will be putting yourself into a much better orbital position.

THRUSTING POWER #8: CELEBRATE YOUR SUCCESSES AND TRACK YOUR ACCOMPLISHMENTS

If you've hit a home run, take time to celebrate a job well done. A celebration can offer much-needed time for recovery after a hard project. It can give credit, where credit is due. One low-cost thank-you is giving personal time off to make up for a period of long hours and intense focus. Another good move is thanking everyone over a meal or during a celebratory get-together. If you have positive feedback from customers or other colleagues, share it at the meeting to reinforce the success of the project. People like to bask in the winning feeling of a job well done, and it can often be more motivating than anything else . . . even a raise. A proper thank you will also help motivate your colleagues to support the next endeavor. If things went well on your project, you might be able to get funding or permission to spend time on another blue-sky project where the team gets to work together again.

It seems like you'll always remember your finest moments in the workplace, but memory fades with time. Your big news of Q1 might fall totally off the radar by Q4. How can you expect your boss to remember your accomplishments if you don't even remember them yourself? That's why it's essential to track the results of projects you've worked on. Keep a running document of all the specific examples that support a case for what a committed team member you are. You can also save emails that give you recognition in a separate email folder so it's easy to find them later. If you have scheduled performance reviews, that's a great time to check your records and make sure you haven't forgotten anything important to present to your boss. If you focused on a personal-growth impact project, your review can also be the perfect opportunity to speak about your accomplishments. A lot of people find that self-improvement conversations come much more naturally in this setting, rather than telling your boss out of the blue that you trained to become a much better presenter.

When you track your results, make sure you save the information long term. If you find yourself gunning for a promotion or looking for a new job, you may need to refer to noteworthy accomplishments from years ago.

THRUSTING POWER #9: ALWAYS BE READY TO TELL YOUR SUCCESS STORY

Be ready for the unexpected. You never know when your boss or CEO will have a few minutes for you to bend their ear, so be primed and prepared when the right time comes up. Even if you've already shared your story, a month from now a senior leader in another department may ask you about your recent work. Or you may find yourself sitting at an airport bar chatting with a VP of a company you've had your eye on for a long time. After you worked so hard driving great results, be able to speak about them at the drop of a hat.

Nikki is the general manager of four hotels in New Orleans. She started as the front desk assistant, was promoted to the front desk manager, then was promoted to the general manager. A key strategy she applied to work her way up was keeping her boss in the loop on all the helpful things she did. Because her boss didn't live in the area, she had to go out of her way to stay on his radar.

When they got a chance to connect on the phone, she told him about the challenges that came up at the hotel and how she handled them. From water leaks to domestic disputes to employees lending room keys out, Nikki was put to the test in many situations. She always made sure her boss knew what happened and how she handled it. Her boss came to know her as a rising star. When he was thinking about selling the hotels and had a buyer interested, he put the buyer in touch with Nikki because he trusted her to give a good impression. He told Nikki that the buyer was a potential investor—not a new potential boss. Nikki did such a great job giving tours of the properties and explaining how she made sure everything ran smoothly that the guy bought the hotels, kept Nikki on staff, and promoted her. Now she manages more than forty employees.[25]

You can keep past accomplishments top of mind by integrating them into your personal brand. I ask my MBA students to illustrate their accomplishments in thirty seconds. That's how they get to develop their personal branding. It's like an elevator pitch. Here's mine.

> I am told I have launched more pharmaceutical blockbuster products than anyone else in the industry, including three $2 billion products. I am also known for leading the charge on more innovation in pharma than probably anyone else: I led this through evangelical selling, the first adherence program, a patient guarantee program, and a patient assistance plan for people who can't afford prescription costs. My night job is adjunct professor at the Fordham Gabelli Business School where I founded the Fordham Leadership Forum.

I've practiced this in the mirror many times, and I'm comfortable saying it. Make sure you do the same thing, continually updating it as your accomplishments build.

MOMENTUM-BUILDING STRATEGIES

Thrust is the force that propels you wherever you want to go. You can have a successful project launch, but you will only rise high if you can generate enough power. Demonstrate all you can, prove you can deliver on your promise and talents, act skillfully—and always follow up with the advice in this chapter. Because getting noticed is the intangible, invisible advantage that lays the foundation for boosting your career. But it doesn't happen out of the blue. Even if you deserve it, you might not get it. Like so much in business, it must be engineered. So play smart and prepare a narrative that makes everyone aware of what you did, how you did it, and what the outcomes are. People will feel the effects, and you will enter a new orbit.

- Create your success story by analyzing the process: write down the opportunities, obstacles, and struggles—and record how you dealt with them.
- Use metrics to measure your results, whether quantitative or qualitative.
- Even if you achieved something that you don't want to broadcast, use your success story to motivate yourself.
- Tailor your message to your audience so that it is heard loud and clear.
- Get feedback before you share results, practice your delivery diligently until you perfect it, and shine yourself up before you take the stage.
- Be ready for pushback and rehearse ways to skillfully respond.
- Stay humble by giving credit where it is due and acknowledging ways you can perform ever better.
- Celebrate every success and track them all, because you never know when a narrative will give you a boost.
- Always be ready to share your success stories.

6

Up Your Speed for a New Orbit

BOOSTING YOUR CAREER IS A JOURNEY THAT you need to navigate skillfully. Your wishes, desires, and efforts for advancement need to align with the vision and goals of other people, the company you work for (or want to work for), and the new role you wish to take on. The whole situation must come together, and for that to happen you need to take all blinders off and accurately assess yourself and your environment.

In the previous chapter, we described the nine ways thrust can get you to an altitude so high that you break out of your current atmosphere. There is so much potential in that moment. To make the most of it and get into orbit—to take on that promotion, or start assigning tasks to your new reports, or begin doing the work you are passionate about—you must up your speed. Odd as it may seem, the way to reach orbital speed is to set aside time for self-reflection and self-improvement.

To get ahead, to this point, *you* set things in motion. But changes don't always happen overnight. In fact, they rarely do. It takes maturity to navigate the big-picture realities of business. New budgets need to be created, reviewed, and passed. Raises and bonuses and promotions need to be planned for. Restructuring a department often takes buy-in from the whole management team. A lateral move might only happen after your current position is filled. If you come unglued, get impatient, or can't hold yourself and all the pieces you've carefully assembled for this effort together, you could harm your mission.

So while you are on your journey, it's vital to stay tuned in to yourself and your personal progress. We've talked a lot about the importance of fueling up with positive relationships. Yes, this includes your multiple real bosses and your network. But the most important relationship you can cultivate is the relationship you have with yourself.

After one hundred days with you on the job, you want HR (ground control) to say, "The best move we've made was promoting (your name) to this position." So look at yourself in a 360-degree way. No one is perfect. There will always be things you need to work on or skills you can further hone. Be wonderfully and brutally honest with yourself. Was or wasn't your performance on your last project better than you imagined? Did some aspects leave you disappointed? What would you do differently if you could do it over?

When you can see areas that need improvement, you empower yourself to become ever better. You will make progress, learn from mistakes, and continue making smart choices that open more opportunities. True self-awareness is how you will find just the right orbital speed. So gauge your personal progress, gauge the environment, and use the tips in this chapter to align the two so that you are moving in sync and getting noticed.

SPEED GAUGE #1: EMPHASIZE STRENGTHS TO OVERCOME WEAKNESSES

Choose how to focus your efforts to improve. In chapter 1, we encouraged you to play to your strengths because tasks related to them feel effortless and pleasurable. These things will undoubtedly come easy for you—but others will be a struggle. It's tough to work day after day in the business environment and not come up against your weaknesses. You may even feel inhibited by them or hopeless about improving them. As someone who wants to make the most of your career, you probably would love to see any weaknesses resolved.

So should you put your time and hard work into improving your strengths or working out your weaknesses? We did a deep dive with HR professionals and C-suite leaders to ponder this thorny question. While lots of pros and cons were shared, we concluded that honing and adding to strengths pays off more than improving weaknesses. The reasoning? It's easier, more beneficial, more productive, and more impactful to become ever better at things you're already great at than to become mediocre at things that are hard for you. Unless you've received a lot of negative feedback about certain weaknesses, and they truly are holding you back, playing to your strengths will garner more return on your efforts. Be reassured: no one is an A+ performer on every track.

It's best to take a well-rounded, big-picture view when facing your strengths and weaknesses. Yes, take time for self-reflection. Yes, consider and act on feedback you gain from others. Just be sure to also think about your situation, your company, and the overall environment. If you're having a really hard time with some of your tasks, or you haven't been able to develop your skills, or you perceive that doing so would stretch you so thin you'd snap, or even sense they go against your innate nature, speak with your boss. Explore how you can take on more projects that play to your strengths rather than your weaknesses. It's much better to proactively bring this up. Don't wait for your boss to somehow perceive the problem herself, because she might interpret it incorrectly. Instead, work together to figure out how you can become most effective and make her look good by harnessing the power of your strengths.

I once managed a terrific client-services person who brought in tons of new business. He was considered a great, productive employee, but he was a terrible manager. People hated working for him; he demotivated them, which meant that his team's overall productivity was much lower than it could be. I had to figure out a solution to better leverage his strengths and prevent the organization from getting burned by his weaknesses. I decided to create a new role for him: strategic officer. It was a position without any direct reports. I moved his team to another manager, and gave him a nice raise to ease the realignment and to acknowledge his strengths.

Although this decision was a win-win for everyone, it would have been much better if the guy had the self-awareness to recognize his own deficiencies, as well as the guts to address them. Before things got bad, he could have easily spoken with me about focusing on what he was really good at—bringing in business. Because when people truly are extraordinary at something that helps the company, bosses want to support them. I would have welcomed the idea and respected him so much more if it had been the result of his own initiative. This example shows how important it is to apply self-reflection to make positive changes.

A lot of people benefit from getting professional help to assess strengths and weaknesses and to figure out how to work with them. Nothing beats meeting with an expert business coach one on one. They offer candid, specific, proactive feedback on how you can leverage your talents. Coaching is popular because it is so productive and energizing. Nowadays there are personal and online coaches for every specialty and every level, so you can benefit whether you're a senior executive, project director, or assistant. Coaches specialize in a wide variety of topics, and you should be able to find someone to help with just about anything, from skills for forming personal connections, to creating harder-hitting presentations, to grooming you for a specific type of advancement, to entering a new corporate culture.

As you move forward with your self-reflection and self-improvement, stay aware of your strengths and weaknesses—but don't let them become the basis for developing limiting beliefs about what you can accomplish. For example, just because math analytics aren't your best subject doesn't mean that you can't manage your department's budget. You may have to work harder and longer and ask a trusted coworker to check your numbers, but it's doable. Basically, if you know of a weakness, build the support or extra time into your plans. Rather than beating yourself up or giving in to failure, you can arrange circumstances so that you succeed. Your boss or a consultant can help with ideas. If you can have general, overall confidence in yourself, you will know that your weaknesses are workable. That could help you try something you don't think you're good at—you just might discover that you can do it when conditions are right.

If you have any type of disability, don't think for a second that it will hold you back from advancing your career and getting what you really want. As a stutterer, I had to work harder than nonstutterers, going up against them for the same jobs. I had to stand out and show that my strengths more than made up for the struggles I had with my speech: I did more research than my peers; I asked better questions; I was more personable in interviews and right after wrote hand-written thank-you notes that got delivered to the office the next day via courier. My drive to stand out in a positive way became a major factor in boosting my career and getting the jobs I wanted. I think my supervisors saw my passion, and it turned into my competitive edge. There are a lot of successful professionals who have conquered other peoples' limiting beliefs about what they could achieve. Jack Chen knows this—he's a brilliant patent attorney who works for Google. He also happens to be blind. If you have a disability, do research on people who have conquered similar challenges and keep them top of mind for daily inspiration.

SPEED GAUGE #2: FIND YOUR NICHE AND BE VALUED FOR IT

Look around your current organization. Think about past jobs you've had. In your self-reflection, take the time to contemplate how people got to be in their roles. Some are tenacious workers who seem to never sleep, others are laid-back conversationalists who take time for people. Some are known for deep product knowledge, others are extremely popular with clients. Some are expert presenters, others . . . well, you're not quite sure what's so great about them. What you'll realize as you do this is that people are different, so they each carve out a niche at an organization. They make themselves valuable in different ways. You want to find your own niche.

Are you the office Excel guru? Or the master of managing productive meetings? Or the person who can close even the toughest prospects? Or the one who can deeply listen to what's hindering progress and suggest a new creative strategy? When you know the types of skills you possess that your colleagues value the most, you can point your efforts toward doing more of that type of work. Developing a unique niche can help you strengthen your personal brand so you get wherever you want to go.

Align What You Offer with What They Need

A niche needs to fit well with your skills and interests and also fill an important need at your organization. Discovering your niche can be a trial-and-error process, but you're probably already well on your way to developing it, even if you haven't been trying to do so.

- Start by identifying what you handle easily that your colleagues either don't know how to do or don't want to do.
- Then imagine if you were to poll ten people you interact with the most at work. What would they say you're great at doing? Looking at yourself from an outside perspective can be a great exercise.

> • Next, ask around. Chances are people will have answers you've never even considered. Getting that feedback can help you understand how you are being valued by coworkers.

Sometimes, you might develop your niche unintentionally. Manuela Stotter is an engineer and LEED project manager, who came upon her niche by simply doing what needed to be done. When she started as a junior at her company, she would take on the things no one else wanted to do. She said her attitude back then was to do what needed to be done—no matter what it was. Even if she had no idea how to do something, or wasn't that interested in finding out, she would volunteer for new tasks. She said this ultimately saved her from being let go during the recession in 2008 when her company went through numerous rounds of lay-offs. "I was doing niche things that no one else knew how to do. If I was to be laid off, my bosses saw there wasn't anyone who had any idea how to do what I did. People more experienced than me and less experienced than me were laid off. It saved me that I took a chance to do things, even getting certified for things, that no one else had proficiency in."

Another benefit Manuela realized by taking on a variety of responsibilities was learning more about what she liked and disliked and better understanding her strengths. Some of the projects Manuela took on over the years didn't seem like a big deal to her, but she realized they were a big deal to her colleagues. Completing the projects came easily enough to her, so she misjudged them as being unimportant. Later, she was surprised to hear her colleagues compliment her on those skills. She came to recognize that to carve out your niche, you just need to be better at something, or know more about something, than other people.[26] When you can specialize in a certain thing, that sets you apart from your colleagues and makes a lasting impression on your bosses.

SPEED GAUGE #3: FIRE UP YOUR CHARISMA TO "SPARK" WITH PEOPLE

Even relationship building is an inside job. Your self-reflection can help identify the best parts of your personality so you can develop them and display them with more confidence. Because a lot depends on genuine emotional connections, whether it's getting promoted or being hired or the extent of acknowledgment you receive. Simply put: if the boss likes another person better than you, he or she will get more attention and opportunities.

If you struggle to "spark" with people, instead of viewing its emphasis as unfair, let it spur self-reflection. Ask yourself: "Why does the other person have a better connection than me?" "What can I do differently to strengthen my relationship with this boss?" Mull over the answers, write them down, update the list as you gather more insight, and then use it to reach out.

Put yourself in your boss's shoes. While his responsibility is to keep the playing field level for the whole team, it can be hard if one person consistently relates with him really well and makes the working experience more enjoyable. Likability is an inescapable factor, and it can seem fair or unfair. It isn't fair when a manager likes someone for reasons that aren't relevant to the workplace, and that happens all too often, but it's understandable when he likes people for the right reasons. Here are some of them: being loyal, dependable, friendly, thoughtful, passionate, enthusiastic, and execution minded. These are all characteristics admirable in employees and people in general.

Manuela interviews job candidates for junior positions at her firm. She looks at education and experience, but given the job level, she knows experience will be limited. That's why she also thinks about cultural fit and what candidates will be like to work with in the long term. "I look for chemistry when I am interviewing, like when you go on a first or second date," she said. She also hires for passion: "I want to see that they want to grow—not that they're just thinking this is a clerical job. If I ask them to do A, will they ask permission to do B, and, thinking out of the box, propose C? Maybe I'll say, 'It's not something I can support,' but I like that they have passion and want to do more than asked. I look for a doer personalities."[27]

Mechele and I think about hiring in the same light. We look for that spark. When we were interviewing editors to help with this book, we had three candidates to choose from. All were talented and had relevant experience, but we felt a stronger emotional connection with one of the candidates. We were drawn to her because she seemed the most excited about our project and she had a sense of humor that felt easy to work with. People who demonstrate passion for their work are almost always more successful than those who are lukewarm, so her enthusiasm made our decision easy.

Mechele is a naturally vivacious person, and that has served her well over the years for building relationships and getting ahead. However, she had to learn to be more direct in letting her enthusiasm show. When she was interviewing years ago at Joseph E. Seagram, then the distilled spirits powerhouse, she could tell the interviewer was interested in her but not *super* interested. Mechele told this to one of her friends who said, "Ask for the job." Mechele didn't know it was appropriate to do that! When she was brought back for another interview with the hiring manager, this time Mechele looked her in the eye and confidently said, "This is the job I want." Mechele could tell that changed everything. And sure enough, she got the job. We now give this advice to people all the time: *Don't forget to ask for the job.* When you say you really want to work for people and their organization, it helps build the emotional connection.

Everyone is seeking approval. All managers want you to want the job, and you can improve your spark at any point in your career. Respond to assignments with enthusiasm, connect tasks to your passions, check in formally or informally, and appreciate feedback.

Use self-reflection to discover why you are excited about what your company does, what your department does, and what you do. Match your drives to your efforts, and do your best to help the company succeed. This positive, genuine can-do attitude is the most powerful way to spark with the people who matter most to your advancement.

SPEED GAUGE #4: STICK WITH THE HEART OF LEADERSHIP—SERVICE

Leadership skills are crucial to moving forward. Whether people report to you or not, a great way to gauge your personal progress is to think about your performance as a leader. Do you lead through example? Have you made things easier for your boss by leading coworkers? How have you supported your direct reports in their career paths? What qualities make you a leader?

The most effective approach to leadership that we've ever come across is an open secret: the best lead by serving others. People feel your good intentions. They respond to you, to share their needs and also to follow your ideas. This focus also helps you stay on the high road as you boost your career so you don't resort to tricks or manipulations or self-aggrandizement. George Bernard Shaw wisely said, "The purpose of life is to have a life of purpose." If you make it a purpose to serve others, your efforts will align with what is most important for your company and your real bosses.

Raymond Dewalt is an F-22 fighter pilot in the US Air Force. He worked incredibly hard to get this highly coveted position, and he notes his success isn't just a result of his flying abilities— it's a reflection of his leadership as well. Raymond prides himself in leading by example. He wants his colleagues to see him working hard because he believes it will inspire them to work hard as well. Performance can be a life or death matter when flying jets that break the sound barrier, so it's essential for everyone to do their very best at all times. "You trust each other with your life and there can't be a weak link. You have to know your job," Raymond said. "You can't be cocky or unapproachable if people have questions. Leaders have to be willing to help others." Cockiness can be a problem for leaders who earn positions that many colleagues are vying for. There are only a couple hundred spots available for fighter pilots, which means only a small percentage of those who set out on the pilot training path end up getting the position they really want. Raymond keeps this in mind, and it helps him put his job in perspective. He feels fortunate to have earned his role, and he is highly motivated to continue demonstrating that he was the right choice. To do this, he focuses on leading by example and supporting his colleagues so they can perform at their best.[28]

Leadership is about service—whether you're in the business of serving your country or not. Good leaders serve all their real bosses: managers, senior leaders, peers, direct reports, clients, customers, HR, and the community. They also serve their company's goals, aligning their personal goals with their company's mission and vision. When you reflect on your progress, see it through this lens of service.

Tamra Feldman is an independent digital marketing and project consultant, so her biggest boss is her clientele. She shows her leadership skills by delivering the consumer engagement outcomes that matter most to her clients. Although Tamra enjoys the vast majority of her work, she realizes that not every task is going to be exciting or intellectually stimulating. She regularly asks herself whether her clients are getting the value they deserve, and whether they are getting their money's worth from the fees she is charging. Sometimes this means that she takes the lead on projects that are unglamorous or tedious. However, that doesn't mean those tasks are unimportant. Tamra always makes her work about doing what needs to be done to serve her clients and help them reach their goals. This perspective has been a key factor in her success with obtaining and retaining nationally recognized clients to grow her business.[29]

This needs to be at the heart of your self-reflections on service: there will be times when doing what's best for the company requires you to put your ego in check. Raymond Dewalt checked cockiness to support the team. Tamra Feldman checked the urge to focus on glamorous tasks in order to fill all the needs her clients have. Earlier in my career, I was tasked with hiring reputable doers, and I quickly realized that enticing quality people to join our struggling agency was a difficult task. I firmly believed that we needed high-level talent to bring in the level of business we wanted. However, to make a competitive offer to these corporate leaders, we had to pay more than originally planned. That meant I had to offer them more money than I was making. Some leaders would not have been able to check their ego and make this move for the betterment of the company. But I knew I was investing in my company's success, which meant investing in my own success as well. It paid off. I took the agency from a forty-person firm to number two in the world.

Never underestimate the power of serving others before serving yourself. Continually self-reflect: clarify your purpose, keep your ego in check, and develop the sincere willingness to do what it takes to give people outcomes they need to succeed.

MOMENTUM-BUILDING STRATEGIES

It takes self-awareness to act skillfully. If you think business is all about doing, it's time for you to pause for reflection. Actions depend on understanding complex situations that include everything in your environment and within you. Even if it happens on your own time, slow down and think about it all. In this chapter, we offered four positive outcomes of this inner grappling. These are ways you can gauge how you're doing and make adjustments. Because the best thing for everyone is for you to become aware of a shortcoming or pitfall before anyone else. So make your career-boosting efforts the genuine results of someone who knows what's up. Take the hits to your ego, because burying your head in the sand is a sure way to get stuck. Instead, embrace business as a journey of developing yourself. That way, as you learn to more accurately perceive the conditions within and without, you can enter any orbit you want to—you can go as far as you have always dreamed of going.

- Self-reflection helps you align yourself with your environment so that the whole atmosphere is mutually supportive.
- As you focus on building your strengths, arrange circumstances to support the areas where you are weak.
- Carve your niche by identifying what you offer that is uniquely appreciated.
- When you develop your charisma, people will spark in their encounters with you and you will make all-important emotional connections.
- Lead your company and your real bosses by staying close to the heart of service.

A Propulsion System for the Long Haul

WHAT DREAM DO YOU HAVE THAT YOU'RE completely unwilling to give up on? Maybe you want a more senior position with additional stock options. To be an industry expert. To develop and bring technologies to market that transform the way we live. To be fully in charge and run the show. To show your children what's possible with passion and perseverance. To challenge yourself to rise as high as you can. Getting there can be a long, arduous journey, so you need a reliable propulsion system. It'll be up to the propulsion system to someday get people to Mars, and you need the equivalent kind of multistaged power sources behind your efforts to boost your career.

Everyone is familiar with the feeling of wanting to give up. When you get that feeling, you need to draw on your power sources. You can do this at any point in your journey, but you especially need it if you have a "deep space" dream that may seem a long way off. As our parting thoughts to send you on your way, we want to offer you seven power sources that you can always turn to. They're reliable, accessible, and incredibly potent methods for giving you the inspirational boost you need.

In the introduction to this book, we said that you can use the advice, tips, projects, and strategies that fill these pages over and over again as you drive your career to yet another level. It's very likely that if you have a deep-space dream, you will need to launch different impact projects many times. You will need to make a variety of meaningful contributions at every stratum, in each atmosphere, and every time you enter a new orbit. Your sources of fuel may likely change as the people around you change, especially if you take a position at a different company or you jump industries. But the seven power sources we offer in this conclusion will stay constant. One or the other will motivate you—no matter what—providing the boost you need to keep journeying.

POWER SOURCE #1: DARE TO DREAM

Whatever the dream, make it nonnegotiable. Doing so has so many benefits: it helps you see what is most important, it cultivates resilience and grit, and you can feel fulfilled on a daily basis as you take steps to get there.

What dream are you unwilling to shelf? Think back to the exercise in chapter 1, where you defined your goals. Did your meaningful impact project help you get closer to reaching them? How far do you still need to go to attain your deep-space dream? You could visualize what the journey ahead might look like. You could plot the ideal steps you would take. You could even consider what stands in your way and how you might overcome these obstacles.

A lot is going to happen that you can't predict. But if your dream is always in mind, it's easy to refine or recalculate the route as you go.

POWER SOURCE #2: WHEN IN NEW TERRITORY, YOU NEED COURAGE

You're advancing your career. So handling new and perplexing situations comes with entering new territory. As we pointed out in chapter 1, you can't stay in your comfort zone if you want to grow in a meaningful way. The people who settle in and coast are the people who get passed over for promotions; they are viewed as mediocre. The people who are always eager to take on more, to learn more, and to challenge themselves are the people who move up. Doing all of these things takes courage.

When I talk with younger employees, such as my MBA students, I can tell they don't always feel ready for the job they really want. Many of them worry that they don't have enough experience or knowledge to manage the challenging projects on the horizon. If you ever feel like this, don't sell yourself short. You've probably heard the saying, "Fake it 'til you make it." A lot of times people say this jokingly, but it's actually great advice. You won't truly learn how to do something without doing it. The people who have the courage to try new things will get the opportunity to learn more and advance.

Heather Hahn has used this philosophy to work her way up the corporate ladder at a variety of companies. She was inspired by an article about the difference between how men and women apply for jobs. The article said that when men read a job description and see five or six things they don't know how to do, they apply for the job anyway. When women read the requirements and there's one thing they don't know how to do, they don't apply. They feel underqualified. That article made a lightbulb go on for Heather because she realized that people apply for stretch positions all the time, and many get hired. She also thought about how this mentality translated to her current role. Why not take on stretch assignments? If her boss needed something done and Heather had never done it before, she wouldn't say she didn't know how to do it—she would say she'd figure it out. "I never act like I don't know what I'm doing, even if I don't," she said with a laugh. She quickly learned that the "I'll figure it out" mentality resonated really well with leaders at her company. "All they wanted was for someone to step up and do their best to help. If I was willing to do that, it didn't matter whether I had experience with that particular task—I was valued."[30] Embracing the unknown with courage builds long-term perseverance. You can jump into a new role, a new company, or a new team—and know you'll figure it out.

POWER SOURCE #3: ALWAYS FEED YOUR MIND MORE

Do everything within your power to continue learning throughout the expanse of your career—and your lifetime. Some people think they know everything, but smart people know they never will. The honest truth is that if you don't keep learning, you will be left behind by your industry and your organization. Things are changing so quickly today that you must be on top, and ahead, of the game.

I firmly believe that leaders aren't born, they are made. That's why I continue to put in the work and read everything I can on leadership and marketing. There are so many great resources out there, so there's no excuse—to grow, read, converse, stay attuned to world events and analyses, watch videos, and listen to audiobooks. Here are some ideas for sources that you can turn to at any time, in any place, as often as you can.

Business Current Events: *Wall Street Journal*, *New York Times*, *Harvard Business Review*, *Forbes*, *Businessweek*, *Wired*, *Fortune*, *Time*, *The Week*

Industry Publications: Industry-specific and role-specific publications let you know about best practices that can support your direct efforts. I read all the pharma periodicals because I do a lot of work in that industry. Since Mechele does marketing for clients in a variety of industries, she reads about all types of businesses—start-ups, manufacturing, staffing, digital, leadership theory, futurism—you name it. The more she reads, the better she understands what her clients are facing at their jobs, and often she gets ideas for how to help them.

Trends and Pop Culture: Marketing is a stimulating field since it is closely related to trends, pop culture, and what's happening in the world. To stay current, Mechele reads up on that kind of news through a variety of outlets. She likes The Moz blog, the *Skimm*, *Quartz*, and *Time* because they publish quick and easy-to-digest versions of top news stories.

Get a Variety of Views: Read a lot of media sources so you gain a variety of perspectives. This is a smart move, since many major news outlets are owned by the same people or influenced by the same advertisers—which absolutely affects the headlines. Mechele recommends reading *The Week US Edition*, because it gives a different perspective by sharing what other countries are publishing about the United States. She also reads media targeted toward different age groups, such as *HuffPo*, Buzzfeed, and Boing Boing because she wants to stay in-the-know about what younger managers are reading. It doesn't stop there—Amy Schumer's new book is currently on her nightstand.

Online Videos: We both highly recommend watching Ted Talks®. These short keynotes are given by some of the best presenters on the planet, in a wide variety of topics. You can watch anything from Brene Brown's *The Power of Vulnerability*, to an eight-talk playlist from various speakers on *The Art of Meaningful Conversation*. If you work from home, try watching a couple of educational talks on your lunch break instead of surfing Instagram. Make sure to watch talks that are related to your industry, as well as those that are seemingly totally unrelated. You can learn so much from watching and listening to great leaders. Then you can embed their advice and wisdom into what you do professionally.

Audiobooks: If you commute, audiobooks are another good option. Mechele loves listening to audiobooks when she's driving because it makes sitting in New York City traffic a little more interesting. Try AudioTech Business Book Summaries or Soundview Executive Book Summaries to hear fifteen- to twenty-minute summaries of new business books.

In addition to unstructured learning, taking a class from a known leader, live or online, can make an impact in your current role or give you the needed boost in your perspective to get ahead. Boning up through a lecture, reading, taking a class, or—best yet—going for a certification will show your boss you're committed to personal career development. Some companies will even reimburse tuition, or at least a portion of it, if the topics covered will help you improve your skills at work. If you can expand your competence, gain enough knowledge, and execute the ideas well, your promotion is a major benefit to your company. For them, it's far more productive and less expensive to fill senior roles when they promote from within.

If you're considering a new career path or a new department within your current organization—but aren't sure if it's right for you—get your toes wet before jumping in. Try a couple of one-hour webinars or a one-day seminar before committing to a new field. There are a variety of free educational resources, such as Kahn Academy, Coursera, Tedx, and Academic Earth, which offer free online coursework from professors at top universities like MIT and Yale. There are also inexpensive audio lectures from real college classes on Audible.com. Mechele recommends Great Courses (available at the library or sold online) to her mentees in part so they can experience what great teaching is, which is unfortunately not so common at many schools.

If you need an official degree or certification, you will probably have to pay unless you are a military veteran. I got my MBA completely paid for on the GI bill. Your company may have a reimbursement policy up to a certain amount. This can be a great way to get an education without breaking into your own piggy bank, if you plan on staying at your organization for the required term after you earn your degree.

If you do plan to go back to school, it can pay off, but balancing a regular workload with classes is not easy. Don't take on more than you can handle while letting your job duties fall by the wayside—that's a surefire way to stall your journey. Also keep in mind that the goal of a business degree is to actually learn something that will help you in your career, rather than just getting an educational experience that looks good on paper. A good education doesn't just teach you things; it teaches you how to think differently. Vetting classes and professors in advance will help you select worthwhile options that can actually change your life, rather than just earn you some letters after your name. Education is a smart investment as long as you're taking the right courses with the right professors, because you take it with you wherever you go.

POWER SOURCE #4: SEE BEYOND CURRENT TRENDS AND STATUS QUOS

Faith Popcorn has a knack for predicting future trends, but people haven't always been receptive to her forecasts. "Believe me, people used to laugh at us when we used to say everything will be home delivered," she said, recalling her consulting experiences. "They're still kind of laughing, because they think brick-and-mortar stores will always be the primary way people shop. I'm telling you right now, Walmart's going to fall; all the drug stores are going to fall. There will be far fewer drugstores because medicine is going to get delivered."[31] That prediction may sound crazy to you, or it may sound as good as looking into a crystal ball. The right mentality is to embrace the idea that even long-standing norms in society change. Just think how Jeff Bezos and Amazon were lightyears ahead of "standard operating procedure" for business . . . and who will disrupt them?

You can train yourself to see norms evolving in the business world. It was always believed that multitasking was the gold standard in productivity. People would even brand themselves as multitaskers, since it was seen as a benefit for any industry or role. Now studies are showing that multitasking makes your brain less effective.[32] The trend of open offices is also on the decline, since people are realizing that it's quite distracting to listen when coworkers sitting right next to you are on the phone. Although this reality is finally widespread enough that the trend is on the wane, people in their gut have known it was true for a long time. If you feel distracted and less effective doing things a certain way, you probably are. This insight isn't rocket science, but it's shocking how often people ignore their instincts and go with the flow of the moment.

As a leader, think critically. No matter what other people think or what the status quo dictates, keep an open mind, listen to what your gut tells you, consider a variety of expert opinions on what's best—professionally and personally—and pay attention to trends as they arrive and go.

POWER SOURCE #5: EVERY FAILURE CAN BECOME AN OPPORTUNITY

With all this advice on succeeding, we can't ignore failing. Anyone who is truly successful has failed—more than once. When you take on a project, not everything is going to go perfectly. Console yourself by knowing that even if you have failed, you are still moving forward. Why? Because you actually learn more from failure than you do from success. Success feels good because your hard work is paid off, but it doesn't rivet your attention like failure does. Failure helps you redirect your course, or direct it more precisely, because you now know where your assumptions were incorrect in something you believed or acted upon. This makes you smarter and more skillful, as you have gained perspective. To turn a failure into a learning moment, reflect on what went wrong until you are able to talk about it objectively, rather than emotionally. Why did things turn out the way they did? What could you have done differently? What was the critical moment?

All of that said, sometimes failure is undeserved. The world, and your playing field in it, is not an inherently fair place. You were coming in early, staying late, going above and beyond for your real bosses, and doing A+ work. How could failure have happened? Maybe the market crashed. Or a competitor beat your timeline. Or the boss had another favorite. Or a scandal happened at the higher levels. It's good to identify the conditions that worked against your success. Because maybe next time, you can be better prepared, see it coming, and ward it off as a show-stopping event. Next time, it could simply be a bump in the road.

When you are legitimately getting passed over, don't ignore it. Ask yourself: Do my boss and colleagues know I am the one who is getting things done? If you aren't gaining recognition, there's a problem—either with your boss's perception of you and your performance or due to an unfair environment in the company. If the damage has already been done, you can address the issue head on. You should always manage up. If you were passed over for a promotion when you truly feel you were the best candidate for the job, approach your boss. Say something like: "I'm happy for Katie because she really wanted that promotion. She'll be great. But I thought I had a chance too. Did anything specifically rule me out?"

Note that you're not acting hurt or angry. You're asking for—and deserve—an honest answer. You may hear a good word: "You're doing a great job, but remember Katie's been here three years longer than you," or "We felt that job wasn't right for you, but something we've been planning may be opening up soon." On the other hand, you may get bad news: for unknown reasons, an unnamed higher-up blocked your promotion. That's upsetting, but at least now you know. You might also find that your boss doesn't have a good reason. Your superiors won't always be A+ players themselves. They may have favorites—liking people based on background, personality, or factors totally unrelated to the job.

When this happens, the question is always, "So now what do I do?" Do you stay? Do you work in more meaningful ways? Do you apply another strategy to become more valued? Even if you do great work, all kinds of circumstances could prevent your advancement. So at times you will wonder whether you should continue to work with these people or move on.

That's a question most of us face at some point or another. The best path depends on your own personal feelings and goals. If you think things are unlikely to get better, you probably won't be very happy if you stay at a job where you aren't treated fairly. There are only so many hours in a day. Are you going to choose to spend them feeling upset, depressed, or angry, instead of moving on to something else? When working with my students at Fordham or my corporate rising-star clients, I tell them that that they are too young to stay in that kind of professional situation. Life is too short to go to work every day and hate what you do, right? So why do it? No matter how much you get paid, you can't work with people who don't appreciate your work or don't like you personally. Start reaching out and move on. Opportunities are always there.

I too have been treated unfairly at work, and it hurt. You can't mope. Tell yourself there is always a better life opportunity, then go out and find it. There are many nasty people in this world, and you're going to meet some of them. As tough as it is, you just need to put things behind you so you can keep moving forward.

One of the best things about failure is that it teaches you resilience. Make the experience of getting passed over for a promotion into something positive. Get out of those doldrums and think of it as an opportunity to grow and develop. It does your psyche good to get up after you've been knocked down, it's a demonstration of your inner strength. Reach out to your contacts and see what else is out there. Consider repurposing or rebranding yourself for the next interview, to get an even better job where you will be appreciated.

Wherever that road takes you, don't be afraid to fail again. Certain people become so fearful of failure that it inhibits them. The fear becomes so ingrained that they don't go to the edge of their limits, put everything they have into the game, or think about how they can do better. That behavior is like giving a second-rate performance. If you try to avoid failure, you will only succeed in limiting your accomplishments. So take it on, and make it work for you.

POWER SOURCE #6: MAINTAIN YOUR BIG-PICTURE VIEW

Building the career you want can create a lot of personal fulfilment. You feel good when you work hard at something, challenge yourself to push your limits, exercise your talents and passions, and contribute to something meaningful. Having a great job also correlates with providing for yourself and your family and leading a stable and enjoyable life. These are the ends to your means.

When you have your nose to the grindstone, it can be easy to lose this holistic perspective on why you're doing the things you do. All too often, people think of happiness as something that will happen as a result of something else. "It'll all be worth it when I get that promotion." Or, "I just have to put in my time and then I'll start liking my job." This is the wrong mentality—happiness and fulfilment are not destinations. If you plan on suddenly arriving there, sorry to say: you won't ever get there. You must enjoy the journey. Sometimes that takes a change in attitude or a serious reprograming of bad habits.

Job stress can be a major factor that limits quality of life. The pace of the working world can sweep you up and make you feel like you have no control. It's essential that you find a way to maintain an even keel, especially when the people around you are stressed out. KaloBios CEO, Dr. Cameron Durrant, spoke to my MBA class at Fordham, and he gave us a lot of helpful advice on maintaining a healthy perspective and fighting back stress. He said when he wakes up in the morning, the first thing he does is think of something he is grateful for in his life. He then spends a couple of minutes focusing on that thing and doing some deep breathing. "When you have gratitude as your base, it's difficult to operate in fear," he counseled.

This is an excellent point, since so many decisions and actions can be affected by worry. For example, you may go into the office early because you are afraid your boss will think less of you if you don't. This is an uncomfortable way to live your life. If you decide you want to go in early, do it because you feel good about it and believe it's the right decision. Do it because you're grateful for the opportunity to demonstrate your dedication.

Dr. Durrant also spoke about maintaining work-life balance and not allowing other people's priorities to eat up the personal time you need and deserve. He said to think about responding to email as someone else's agenda. To illustrate his point, he noted that now that everyone has smartphones, it has become a habit that people continually check email and texts and feel obligated to respond promptly, regardless of the time of day. "The monkey that's on their back goes onto your back the moment you open your email. To deal with that stressor, you need to be in a good place. You owe it to yourself, and to the people who are requesting you to do things, to be in a centered place before you deal with it." And as many experts Mechele has interviewed have advised, you need to claim back your prerogative to answer or pass on it for the time being. Calmer people, centered people, don't jump up to reply to every probe and request.

Work-life balance is crucial not only for morale but also for maintaining productivity and avoiding burnout. Constant hard work and long hours are not sustainable in the long term. People need time to relax and hang with family and friends. When you take time away from work, your mind can reset so that you have a fresh perspective when you return. This is often all you need to find clever solutions to workplace challenges.

The Basics of Balance

Here are some ways to combat stress and maintain a holistic perspective in your life. Could you add any of the following strategies to your routine?

- Keep in regular contact with family and friends you can lean on as a support network.
- Surround yourself with positive and caring people.
- Practice mindfulness and deep breathing exercises.
- Get plenty of sleep, at least seven hours.
- Eat healthy.
- Exercise regularly.
- Practice gratitude.
- Seek to explore and have an adventure at least every week.
- Find some hobbies, like tennis, golf, painting, or museums.

Also remember that your reports need personal time. Be supportive of their work-life balance, and measure performance based on outcomes rather than just time spent on the job. When your employees feel freer, it actually keeps them closer.

POWER SOURCE #7: PERSONAL INTEGRITY IS YOUR AXIS

The last thing that Mechele and I would like to leave you with is an important one. As you work to make an impact, gain recognition, and boost your career, don't ever lose your integrity. There are many examples of people who have made their way to the top by lying, cheating, or treating others poorly. This sends the message that it's okay to behave that way—when nothing could be further from the truth. Doing good in the world is something that always has value and pays forward throughout your life—more value than getting promoted. When you look back on your life, you want to feel good about what you accomplished. What legacy are you building? How will people remember you? Set an example you can feel proud of.

In this book, we set out to share with you all the unspoken secrets to getting ahead. Some of them may strike you as revolutionary. Before you get too excited about their potential, put them into practice and watch them work for you. Some of them may strike you as common business sense. Just don't take these too lightly, because while you know them, you might not be applying them. Do yourself a favor—do your career a favor—and benefit from the vast experience we drew on to create this guide. We're proud to have been your mentors, and our hope is that you will use this book to build the career you were reaching for in the same way people once reached for the stars.

So, what's your next impact project?

Notes

1   Never-ending performance reviews by Justin Fox. Best Columns: Business. *The Week.* August 25, 2016.

2   Faith Popcorn, speaker at Fordham Leadership Forum class taught by Sander. Fordham Gabelli School of Business. November 3, 2011.

3   John D. Mayer (2008). "Human Abilities: Emotional Intelligence." *Annual Review of Psychology.* 59: 507–536. DOI: 10.1146/annurev.psych.59.103006.093646.

4   Dr. Cameron Durrant, speaker at Fordham Leadership Forum class taught by Sander. Fordham Gabelli School of Business. September 28, 2016.

5   Neil Irwin. "How to Become a C.E.O.? The Quickest Path Is a Winding One." *The New York Times.* September 9, 2016. http://www.nytimes.com/2016/09/11/upshot/how-to-become-a-ceo-the-quickest-path-is-a-winding-one.html?emc=eta1&_r=0.

6   Elizabeth Dunn and Michael Norton, *Happy Money: The Science of Smarter Spending* (New York: Simon & Schuster, 2013).

7   Chaoming Song, Zehui Qu, Nicholas Blumm, and Albert-László Barabási. "Limits of Predictability in Human Mobility." *Science.* February 19, 2010: Vol. 327, no. 5968, pp. 1,018–1,021. DOI: 10.1126/science.1177170.

8   Ramon Vullings and Marc Heleven. *Not Invented Here: Cross-Industry Innovation.* (Amsterdam, The Netherlands: BIS Publishers, 2015).

9   Madanmohan Rao, research director at YourStory Media, regarding cross-industry innovation as depicted in *Not Invented Here,* September 16, 2015.

10   Austin Kleon. *Steal Like an Artist: 10 Things Nobody Told You About Being Creative*. (New York: Workman Publishing Company, 2012), p. 36.

11   Ibid, p. 21.

12   Pamela Meyer. *From Workplace to Playspace*. (San Francisco, CA: Jossey-Bass, 2010).

13   Phone interview with Heather Hahn, July 8, 2016.

14   https://www.ted.com/talks/dan_ariely_what_makes_us_feel_good_about_our_work.

15   Phone interview with Tom Randall, July 28, 2016.

16   Phyllis Korkki. "What Could I Possibly Learn from a Mentor Half My Age? Plenty." *The New York Times*. September 10, 2016. http://www.nytimes.com/2016/09/11/business/what-could-i-possibly-learn-from-a-mentor-half-my-age.html?emc=eta1.

17   Phone interview, July 7, 2016.

18   In-person interview, August 9, 2016.

19   In-person interview, August 10, 2016

20   HR Solutions, 2011.

21   Dale Carnegie. *How to Win Friends and Influence People*. (New York: Simon and Schuster, 1964).

22   Interview with Congresswoman Rice in the Fordham Lecture Series, February 18, 2016. http://www.flaumnavigators.com/interviewing-congresswoman-rice-in-the-fordham-leadership-lecture-series.

23   Sander A. Flaum. "Shade-Tree Syndrome." PharmExec.com. Oct 1, 2007. http://www.pharmexec.com/shade-tree-syndrome.

24   Paul Ingrassia. "Hail, Mary." *Fortune* magazine. September 15, 2016, p. 85.

25   Phone interview, July 13, 2016.

26   Phone interview, October 11, 2016

27   Ibid.

28   Phone interview, July 13, 2016 (pseudonym used).

29   Phone interview, October 10, 2016.

30   Phone interview, July 8, 2016.

31   Faith Popcorn, Fordham Leadership Forum.

32   Nancy K. Napier. "The Myth of Multitasking." *Psychology Today*. May 12, 2014. https://www.psychologytoday.com/blog/creativity-without-borders/201405/the-myth-multi-tasking.

Acknowledgments

Boost Your Career: How to Make an Impact, Get Recognition, and Build the Career You Want is the result of years of coaching that motivated me, together with my wonderful and talented wife and partner, Mechele, to write. We've mentored scores of young leaders on ways to move forward by making notable impacts within their units and departments. The book's advice evolved from the combination of coaching MBA students and the "rising stars" within my client organizations, and many years first as a corporate marketing head, then running a global ad agency, then starting my own consulting business, and most importantly, my tenure as an adjunct professor of Leadership Studies at the Fordham University Gabelli School of Business in New York City. My "boost your career" lessons were learned climbing the corporate ladder and building Becker, Euro RSCG (now Havas Health) to number two globally. I was fortunate to have some great mentors to guide me through that rocky road, and we urge all our readers to find their own mentors. Having engaged advisors around you is paramount in boosting your career.

Much help went into producing this book. The interviews came from a range of exceptional people, including great leaders who offered their experiences with coaching "rising stars." Our deep thanks to our interviewees, who were candid and shared their experience in the art and craft of gaining recognition through self-reflection, courage, and openness to taking on the mantle of leadership. Thanks to Dean Donna Rappacioli at Fordham for her unwavering support of the Fordham Leadership Forum and to my students for their inspiration and deep interest in being great at their jobs.

Mechele and I are indebted to Amelia Forczak for her belief in our concept and writing talent. Our book agent, hard-working Dabney Rice of Dupree Miller, was incredibly helpful in introducing us to our publisher and our talented editor there, Kelsie Besaw. And more thanks to Jan Miller and Shannon Marvin at Dupree Miller. Finally, our gratitude to Jennifer Holder who helped so much to crystallize our manuscript and bring out, as John Glenn would say, its earthly experience.

Index

Books from Allworth Press

Brand Thinking and Other Noble Pursuits
by Debbie Millman with Rob Walker (6 x 9, 336 pages, paperback, $19.95)

Corporate Creativity
by Thomas Lockwood and Thomas Walton (6 x 9, 256 pages, paperback, $24.95)

Emotional Branding
by Marc Gobe (6 x 9, 352 pages, paperback, $19.95)

From Idea to Exit
by Jeffrey Weber (6 x 9, 272 pages, paperback, $19.95)

Infectious
by Achim Nowak (5½ x 8¼, 224 pages, paperback, $19.95)

Intentional Leadership
by Jane A. G. Kise (7 x 10, 224 pages, paperback, $19.95)

Millennial Rules
by T. Scott Gross (6 x 9, 176 pages, paperback, $16.95)

Peak Business Performance Under Pressure
by Bill Driscoll and Peter Joffre Nye with John McCain (6 x 9, 224 pages, paperback, $19.95)

The Pocket Small Business Owner's Guide to Business Plans
by Brian Hill and Dee Power (5¼ x 8¼, 224 pages, paperback, $14.95)

Positively Outrageous Service
by T. Scott Gross (6 x 9, 224 pages, paperback, $19.99)

Star Brands
by Carolina Rogoll with Debbie Millman (6 x 9, 256 pages, paperback, $24.99)

The Ultimate Guide to Internships
by Eric Woodard (6 x 9, 280 pages, paperback, $14.99)

Website Branding for Small Businesses
by Nathalie Nahai (6 x 9, 288 pages, paperback, $19.95)

To see our complete catalog or to order online, please visit www.allworth.com.